RICHARD P...

This Ca... ...ives!

WITHDRAWN

W9-BYU-877

RICHARD PRYOR

This Cat's Got 9 Lives!

by
Fred Robbins
and
David Ragan

A Delilah Book
distributed by G.P. Putnam's Sons
NEW YORK

First printing 1982/Second printing 1982

ISBN: 0-933328-14-1

Library of Congress Catalog Card Number: 81-67654

Delilah Books
Delilah Communications
118 E. 25th Street
New York, N.Y. 10010

Manufactured in the United States

Special thanks to Lou Drozen and Laff Records.
For more information about the Laff Records comedy recordings,
they are located at 4218 West Jefferson Blvd., Los Angeles, Ca., 90016.

Book and cover design by Ed Caraeff.

ACKNOWLEDGMENTS

FOR THEIR HELPFUL ASSISTANCE ON THIS BOOK, THE AUTHORS WOULD
LIKE TO EXPRESS THEIR GRATITUDE TO: Dan Aykroyd, Wendy Bane,
David Brenner, George Carlin, Rob Cohen, Bruce Jay Friedman, Budd Friedman,
Leonard Gaines, Sally Hanson, Buck Henry, Lena Horne, Gerald Jackson,
Robert Klein, Howard W. Koch, Cleavon Little, Sidney Lumet, Tod Mesrow
of WTTW, Eric Naumann, Joel Oliansky, Joan Rivers, Edgar Rosenberg,
Paul Schrader, Michael Schultz, Cicely Tyson and Barbara Walters
and Barwell Productions, Inc.

DEDICATION

For Gregory Reynolds, a young friend.

—David Ragan

To Ingrid, for her patience . . . . And to Bert Williams, Pigmeat Markham, Lenny Bruce and all the others who paid such heavy dues and paved the way.

—Fred Robbins

Table of Contents

1.

Take One:

RICHARD PRYOR IS NOT YOUR AVERAGE NIGG. . . . Hold it! Stop right there. Back up and back off. You're trespassing on private property. That word, lingering but dying on the vine before he restored it to vigorous life, is his now, stamped with his registered trademark. Only he knows how to hold and handle, defuse and denature, burnish and brandish it. It is still a mean and ugly word in the hands of others, even those who would use it hyperbolically to get a book about him off to an eyebrow-raising start.

Take Two:

RICHARD PRYOR IS NOT YOUR AVERAGE COMIC, comedian, joke-teller, funnyman, clown, jester, buffoon, wit, humorist, gagman, classic fool, actor, performer, player, Thespian, trouper, movie star, recording artist, pantomimist, harlequin, tragedian, or mummer.

Richard Pryor, to the nth degree, is all of these—and a few things more.

Way back in 1977, one of his directors, Paul Schrader, who helmed *Blue Collar*, paid him what was then the ultimate compliment: "I feel quite strongly that Richard will be the biggest black actor *ever*."

Strike the word "black." It no longer applies.

An actor who can command a picture fee of three million dollars plus thirty-four percent of the gross receipts of a film is not only past being labeled by color, but is outrunning every other superstar on today's uncrowded field—Burt Reynolds, Marlon Brando, Goldie Hawn, Robert Redford, Paul Newman, Barbra Streisand, Bill Murray or Robert DeNiro.

Pryor not only outearns any star on the list, he also makes many more films. Witness his 1982 work schedule: his second concert film, *Live on the Sunset Strip*, *The Toy*, co-starring Jackie Gleason, *Color Man*, *Superman III*, in which he plays the villain, and *The Charlie Parker Story*.

Perhaps Richard Pryor looms so large because he is perpetually and perennially the reinvented man, who, without leav-

Man on Fire

ing this life, or losing any prior hard-won knowledge, seems reincarnated each time one focuses upon him.

The directionless Peoria kid gave way to the ambitious young stand-up comic who wanted to be the wildly acerbic Lenny Bruce but settled for being the carbon copy of the amiable Bill Cosby. Shedding that coat, he evolved as the outrageous and controversial comic who was almost as well known for his self-destructive impulses and drug abuse as for his scatalogical humor.

He was less than secretive about his drug habits. "I love drugs. I do. I really do," he proclaimed. "I like drugs, and I don't want to say it, like, to make other people want to do 'em. I really want to say that. But I like some cocaine every now and then. Sit around with my friends and get high. I mean I enjoy that."

Talking about his early years in Peoria, Pryor once said, "I always felt I was the child protégé of the neighborhood because they wouldn't let me get into stuff. No dope! I first smoked a reefer when I was twenty years old." Once introduced to drugs, though, he made up for lost time. Soon they had become a major factor in his life. Marijuana, however, proved to be just a passing fancy, because he said, "I can't smoke it. I get paranoid." Nor was he snagged by heroin. As he once told reporter Ace Burgess, "There's nobody in the world who can't get hooked on heroin. If you fuck with it you're going to get hooked. And if you're hooked, there's nothing you can do about it, except get off." But, Cole Porter's lyrics to the contrary, he got quite a kick out of cocaine.

Between 1967 and 1970 he earned $250,000. Most of it, reportedly, went to support his love affair with coke. When he dropped out of the big leagues of show business in '70 and began playing small clubs in Berkeley, California, one reason for choosing that locale was because cocaine was easy to get there. "I'd take the dope and pretend I was Miles Davis," he has said. "But I couldn't have been a junkie because when I wanted to stop I stopped on a dime."

He quit for a while in 1976 ("I'm a grown man; I got tired of it"), a year or so after a noted black lawyer from Atlanta, David Franklin, a counselor to former UN Ambassador Andrew

Young, began handling his business affairs. It is said that Pryor credited Franklin with saving his financial life, helping him get out from under $600,000 in debts. It is also reported that the lawyer laid it on the line to him about drugs. "I told him," Franklin has been quoted as saying, "that I wasn't interested in representing a junkie."

A 1977 *Newsweek* piece on Pryor also contained this observation from David Franklin, who handles many black show business notables: "Ninety percent of the black artists are getting ripped off today. The best service I could give them would be to take a machine gun and wipe out all the people around them and start over."

Before any such drastic action was taken, Pryor and the lawyer parted company, acrimoniously on the comic's part. In March 1981, Pryor sued his former manager for alleged mismanagement of funds.

He alleged that David Franklin, who once received a Rolls Royce from him as a gift, mixed "hundreds of thousands" of Pryor's dollars with those of other people. In the suit he also claimed that the lawyer kept poor records and wrote "hundreds of checks" without stating the reason or "whose funds were being used." More recently, when a reporter sought to get the lawyer's side of the story and phoned his firm in Georgia, a spokesperson at his office said, "Mr. Franklin feels that, when someone is suing you for a million dollars, it is wise to make no comment."

While off cocaine, Richard Pryor was urged to speak before youth groups on the dangers of the drug. He refused, saying, "I'd feel hypocritical because I like cocaine very much. I'd feel stupid if I told people not to do it, because people like what it does. I can't get up and preach about it. I wouldn't want to tell nobody no lie. I could only tell them what it did to me. It *fucked me up.*"

Then he cautiously added another reason for his silence: "I might do it again."

He went back to cocaine.

Then came The Fire.

Presto! Chango! Out of the flashing flames and smoke, a phoenix arises from the ashes, a really new Richard Pryor.

On the day he was burned, June 9, 1980, he was halfway through the production of the movie *Bustin' Loose*. Staging a recovery that was little short of miraculous, he returned to the studio less than three months later to finish the film, amid reports that more had changed than his appearance.

Not everyone believed it.

One unconvinced reporter asked Michael Schultz, who knows the actor well and has directed him in other pictures besides *Bustin' Loose*, if the stories about the "new" Richard Pryor were true.

"Oh, definitely," Schultz answered. "All you have to do is look at his face. When we started on *Bustin' Loose*, Richard was really on the downhill side. He was drinking heavily [a fifth of whiskey a day, Pryor has said] and using coke, and all the rest. Everything he was doing he was doing to total excess. Trying to really cash in the chips.

"When he came back to finish the picture, after the fire, we saw a totally different Richard Pryor. Forty pounds lighter. Visibly scarred. In very frail physical condition. The first work we did when he returned was some 'looping,' putting new words over the old prints. Up on the screen was a Richard Pryor that was heavily overweight and puffed from excessive alcohol. Richard looked at himself on the screen and tears came to his eyes. He had to stop. Then he looked off and said, 'Thank you, God, for all your poor creatures.' And he talked about himself as if it was somebody totally different, some other person outside of himself. The accident really brought him around to seeing the beauty of things, instead of trying to destroy it. And he counts his birthday now as the day of the fire."

Howard Koch, producer of Pryor's later *Some Kind of Hero*, reports, "One time I heard one of the guys on the set ask him where he was born. He said, 'The Sherman Oaks Burns Center.' "

"The person I worked with before the accident and the person I worked with after it appeared to me to be two different people," says *Bustin' Loose* co-star Cicely Tyson. "Afterwards, he seemed a lot more peaceful. He did not seem as tortured to me. I think all of the things that we tend to do in our lives are an outcry for love, really, things that we sometimes do to ourselves, what appears to be destructive and negative. And sometimes it reaches sheer desperation. I think that's what happened in his case. And I believe the outpouring of love that he got, by mail and from his friends, the assurance that, yes, he is loved by millions of people all over the world, is what gave him a certain peace. Also, I feel that nothing can be more sobering than being that close to death and surviving."

Few men have ever come so close to death as Richard Pryor and lived.

Now, predictably, since much of his comedy derives from his pain, Pryor has turned that tragedy into humor, saying, "I want to set the record straight. I was having cookies and milk and I mixed homogenized and low fat milk and I dropped in the cookie and it blew up."

He also jests that the fire caused him to change in these ways: "You stay away from fireplaces. You will not go on the Fourth of July picnic. And you refuse to use gas in your car. You get electric motors."

But he also says, sincerely, "I'm grateful for the fire. It saved my life. I believe that in about three months I would have been dead. I was just going down, inside, you know. Depression. And I just think I would have been dead or in an institution. Now, I don't go to church or nothing, but I feel born again. I feel like God has given me a second chance in life."

It is a second chance he did not expect to be given on that summer night when he ran screaming from his house in the northwest area of the San Fernando Valley.

"I was running because I didn't want to die sitting down," he would live to tell Barbara Walters on TV seven weeks later. "I tried to run so I could bust my heart. I just wanted to run out. I didn't want to die sitting there waiting on an ambulance."

Hearing his screams and seeing him as he fled, a woman neighbor telephoned for help, telling the emergency operator, "A man is running down the street and he's on fire."

A fire department rescue ambulance raced to the scene and found him wandering in a daze more than a mile from his home. "By that time, the flames were out, but he was in a lot of pain," they reported. "He was wearing khaki trousers, but whatever else he'd been wearing on top was completely gone."

He was rushed to the Sherman Oaks Burn Center, where examining doctors ascertained that he'd suffered third degree burns over the entire upper half of his body. His chest, abdomen, back, hands and face were badly damaged. And, medical authorities ominously observed that only twenty-five to thirty-five percent of people in his age group ever survived burns so extensive.

As quickly as the flames had enveloped him, turning him into a human torch, rumors swept through Hollywood and then across the nation that, at the time of the accident, he had been freebasing; heating a base of cocaine and ether in the bowl of a pipe with a butane torch, and then inhaling its highly concentrated vapors.

When he had recovered, Pryor denied this tale. Explaining what had really happened that night, he said, "I had been up for about five days straight, and on the first three days I *had* been freebasing. That's the truth. But I'd decided I wasn't going to do it anymore. On the night that I got burned, my partner and I were sitting in my bedroom drinking rum – this Jamaican rum called Overproof – and talking about life. I wasn't on drugs then. Somehow I knocked over the bottle and spilled some of the rum. My partner went to get a towel out of the bathroom and we started cleaning up the spilled rum. Then we tried to light cigarettes and the lighters wouldn't work. You know how you go to someone's house and they have those lighters sitting on the table and they don't work? So I said, 'Get all the lighters, every lighter in the house.' We were cleaning them and filling them up. Then I started to light a cigarette and one of them did work. The next thing I knew I was on fire. I heard a noise like 'Pow!' and suddenly I was engulfed in flames. That's all I remember."

Then he added, to an *Ebony* editor, "Look, I know that the fact that I admit that I'd been freebasing several days before the fire will make people wonder if I was also doing it that night. But there were no drugs involved with that incident. Actually, the connection had fucked up and didn't get there, so I didn't have any coke to freebase. That's the truth."

After emergency surgery at the Sherman Oaks Community Hospital Burn Center, doctors gave him only one chance in three to survive.

Three days after the fire, Dr. Richard Grossman, of the Center, said, "I'm a little more pleased with his condition today. But I still don't give him more than a fifty–fifty chance. It's still a guarded outlook for a man of his age, his condition and all the junk he's put in his body."

Wrapped in gauze soaked with silver sulfadiazene, which fights infection, and lying on "egg crates," a soft material constructed of a series of cones to lessen pressure on the skin, Richard Pryor fought to live.

He asked for just one person to be with him throughout his ordeal, his friend, actor and former football star Jim Brown. Afterwards, with tears in his eyes, he would speak of Brown's "love" and "his caring." "For three hard weeks he was there," he would say. "When I went to sleep, he was there. When I woke up, he was there. And I kept saying to myself, 'I can't give in to the pain . . . not in front of Jim Brown.' "

His struggle to survive was valiant – and agonizing. While willing himself to live, he also surrendered himself into the hands of his doctors. Several times a day he was moved into a whirlpool bath, where hot water and antiseptics washed over his body. Twice a day, up to two hours at a time, he was in a hyperbaric high-pressure oxygen chamber, where pure oxygen is forced into the body to retard scarring and help speed healing of the skin. He underwent debridement, an excruciating surgical procedure in which burned skin is removed from the body, exposing raw skin and nerves. He withstood three painful skin grafts in which thin strips of undamaged skin were removed from his thighs and calves to replace burnt tissue on his upper body. He survived a siege of pneumonia and kidney complications, and underwent plastic surgery.

Through it all, he prayed. "Nobody ever considers burning up," he said. "It's something you just don't ever think about, and then all of a sudden there you are, burning up. And, you know, you don't call on the Bank of America to help you. You don't call on nobody but God. Dear Jesus! Lord! My Master! You know, all those people, those names you'd forgotten."

"I never knew so many folks cared," he said as thousands of get-well cards, telegrams, phone calls and floral gifts flooded the hospital. Besides unknown admirers, the well-wishers encompassed a Who's Who of the world's most celebrated persons: Ted Kennedy, Muhammad Ali, Chevy Chase, John Anderson, California Governor Edmund Brown Jr., Sammy Davis Jr., Johnny Carson, Sidney Poitier, and more. Perhaps the telegram, accompanied by flowers, which most delighted him was that from his old friend Redd Foxx: "I knew you were looking for me, but I didn't expect you to send up smoke signals."

All these helped speed Pryor's recovery. So, too, did another weapon in his survival arsenal – his own courageous sense of humor.

Two weeks after the burn, Jim Brown was able to report: "He's been joking and kidding. He's sharp as a tack – telling ten jokes a minute. He says, 'I can always open a flower shop if the doctors don't let me go back to work right away.' "

From the beginning, physicians restricted his visitors to immediate family members – his children and his estranged wife Deboragh – and a few close friends, actor Stan Shaw (a daily visitor), Redd Foxx, Bill Cosby, Elliott Gould, Sammy Davis Jr., and Cicely Tyson, among others.

Interestingly, in retrospect, the one friend not allowed to visit him, at least in the early weeks of his hospitalization, was Jennifer Lee.

Dark-haired and beautiful, Jennifer Lee is a well-to-do WASP from Cropseyville, in upstate New York, where her father is an attorney. And she is a young woman of many facets. A talented actress, she made her movie debut in a leading role in

1974's *Act of Vengeance*, and later played Walter Matthau's daughter-in-law in *The Sunshine Boys*. She is a composer and has written songs for several films. She is an interior decorator who once helped furnish and decorate Pryor's Northridge, California mansion. And, before and after his 1977 marriage to Deboragh McGuire, Jennifer Lee was also the main lady in his life.

But the course of their love did not run smoothly.

Early in 1979, she appeared with him on television when Barbara Walters visited them at Pryor's showcase of a home. When Walters asked the comedian if he'd want to marry again, he said, "Maybe. I like to have a family. I'd like to have a family where I could be with Jennifer." He said that Jennifer had made a difference in his life. Asked how, he answered, "Because she came to me when I was in need, and she stood by me through a lot of pain, when most people walked away from me, and thought it was over. And I loved her, and she loved me, and we got to love each other, for real. Not just the word part, we went through that part, too, you know. And we went through all the racism together; found out that we really have souls and we were people."

Earlier on the day of the fire, Jennifer had been with Pryor. But she had gone back to her own apartment before the accident.

When he was in the hospital, though, he did not want to see this woman to whom he'd always paid tribute in his appearances, calling her "the greatest influence in my life—the most positive." Reportedly, he preferred that she not see him in the early stages of his recuperation.

Next to Jim Brown, however, no one kept such constant vigil at the hospital as Jennifer.

Through Jim Brown, a mutual friend, she was able to communicate with Pryor through notes and send him verbal messages. "I love him with all my heart," she said. "He is the most wonderful person in the world. But the doctors say I cannot visit with him until he is completely out of danger. So I'm just going to hang in here now, and keep reminding him of how much I love him."

Another regular visitor at the hospital was one of the comic's ex-wives, Maxine. And oddly enough, it was she who finally arranged for Jennifer to see him.

Says actor Leonard Gaines, a friend of both Maxine and Pryor, "Maxine likes Jennifer, thinks she's a good chick. And she was very good to Jennifer. Sneaked her into the hospital. Dot-dot-dot. Then he finally wound up marrying Jennifer."

On July 23, 1980, on the day of his release from the hospital, Barbara Walters taped another interview with Richard Pryor, which was shown on ABC on August 5. Originally, Walters had planned merely to repeat their previous talk-session. But, tracking the newswoman down at the Republican convention, Pryor suggested another camera confrontation, in which he might discuss the changes the fire experience had wrought in his life.

As a lead-in to this new segment, Barbara Walters first screened the interview they did early in 1979. Segueing from the old to the new conversation, she observed elliptically, "That was Richard Pryor a year and a half ago. Since then he and Jennifer broke up, causing him much personal pain." Jennifer was not mentioned again.

About the same time as he talked to Barbara Walters, Pryor granted an extensive interview to Charles L. Sanders, which appeared in *Ebony* Magazine.

Asked if he and Jennifer Lee were still together, the actor answered: "Uh, no. We were. I thought we were friends, but that's what *I* thought. Obviously I should have stopped and asked her what *she* thought. But I care about her, too. She helped me pull through, because when I first met her I was . . . whew! . . man, I was at a low point."

But Richard Pryor, as he has said . himself, is a "man of many layers, many levels"–and, it might be added, many surprises and contradictions.

Back in 1976, he flatly declared, "I would never marry another white woman. No, I wouldn't. I've been there. It's too hard."

He changed his mind. In mid-August 1981, in a secret ceremony in Hawaii, when everyone thought their romance was over, he married Jennifer Lee.

"There may be some prejudice from black people that I am married to a white woman," he said. "But I don't understand that. I think that people ought to at least have the right to make love to whomever they want to make love to. You know what I mean? The important thing is that a man reaches a certain point in his life when he needs a comforting woman. It doesn't matter what color that person happens to be if she's got that necessary factor for his happiness."

Soon after leaving the hospital, a now drug-free Pryor left his Northridge mansion and moved to the quiet of a fenced-in, five-acre estate on the wild side of the island of Maui in Hawaii, a spot he had visited before the fire, when on his honeymoon with Deboragh McGuire.

Upon first reflection, this seems an odd locale in which to picture Richard Pryor, the peripatetic man who once said, "I want to relax and find out what I want to do with my life. Trouble is, I don't know how to relax. People tell me, 'You ought to just lie on the beach and close your eyes.' I can't do that. I gotta keep one eye open out of fear that somebody is gonna sneak up and hit me with a board."

Privacy is what he sought and has found in the small tropical rain forest settlement near Hana. The road to the main side of Maui is in such disrepair that it takes all day to make the journey. An expert pilot, Pryor flies back and forth, or to Honolulu when he must, at the controls of his single-engine Grumman.

Living with Jennifer in a modest one-bedroom house with an arresting view of the coastline, the comedian-actor spends many leisurely hours fishing off a pier or touring the island on a moped. Here also, he put the finishing touches on his autobiography, *Up From the Ashes*.

"I haven't met anyone here who's strange," he has said. "There's no wickedness. I went to a festival once and watched them dance. It was so pure and innocent. And they brought children. I like that. When I first saw this place again, I cried. I thanked God for letting me live to see it."

One visitor has euphorically described his current setting as "a calm paradise—sun-baked, sun-dazzled, with days that drip like molasses, sunsets with double rainbows and thousands of miles of ocean."

As isolated as the area is, Pryor has a number of famous, but distant, neighbors such as Kris Kristofferson and George Harrison, who escape to this tropical retreat whenever they can, and Carol Burnett, who lives there year-round.

When told that Burt Reynolds also had purchased acreage down the road from him in Hana, Pryor cracked, "There goes the neighborhood."

Certainly the fire that almost destroyed Richard Pryor had made him a new man. As one friend says, "He's so happy he doesn't know which way to go with it. He thanks God every day."

But some have expressed concern about the comedic future of a gentled Richard Pryor.

Not to worry, insists Rob Cohen, producer of two of his films.

"His accident had a great impact on him," says Cohen. "I think that was the turning point for him. He was building up to a point where all the reasons he got there were no longer apropos. It's a crazy thing with comedians like Richard and Woody Allen.

They get successful by tapping their neuroses. Whatever their hangups, fuckups and short circuits are, they observe and make fun of them, and people love them for it. Originally, Richard was fueled by a lot of anger – anger at white people, anger at the white establishment, love and compassion for black people but also pity for their supposed helplessness, or alcoholism or drug abuse, or whatever. And, as he got more successful he began to lose his way. And the drug thing, I think, filled in the gaps. Once he came to the brink of death, which he had been playing with in many ways for a long time, I think he saw that he hated it. And he got himself fucked up in the perfect way – a funny way, a painful way – where he was conscious through the whole thing and he could really understand what it was like to destroy himself. Once that happened, and once he saw the way people rallied around him, it gave him a new perspective on life. And I think it's going to do nothing but make him a greater and more enriched artist."

2.

SOMETHING THERE IS THAT DOESN'T LOVE MODern American comedians. Not those of the truth-speaking variety. Something there is that hounds them, and hunts them down, and unless they are strong, that something sometimes kills them.

Richard Pryor may consider himself fortunate. For he is strong; strong enough to have already survived most of the pressures that destroyed Freddie Prinze and particularly Lenny Bruce, the angry, violent screamer from the acid gut.

A pioneer crusader against false values, ahead of his time (the arch-conservative '50s and early '60s) and aware of the risk he was taking, Lenny Bruce seemingly invited the wrath of the gods.

After years of emceeing in strip joints, Bruce gained notoriety in clubs by assaulting the sexual, racial and religious taboos of an uptight generation through the use of "forbidden" words: motherfucker, cocksucker, shit, fuck, pussy, piss, cock, asshole, screw, jack-off. For the rest, see Eric Partridge's *Dictionary of Slang and Unconventional English.*

"They" were lying in wait for him. First, they pricked him. To Broadway columnist Louis Sobol, Lenny Bruce was no more than a "dirty humorist, cleverly spewing out his four-letter smut." While another critic labeled him "a sad, sick, self-destructive genius." Then an outraged Establishment rose in fury against him and got him arrested—five times in a single year in California. Finally unable to control him, as his club act grew more frank, more scatalogical, more political, they jailed him. "Don't take away my words!" he begged the judge. The judge did take them away, and his freedom. Four months in a New York workhouse. The charge: obscenity.

All was downhill for Lenny Bruce after that. Hounded beyond human endurance, he became deranged—living like a caged animal in his house in the Hollywood hills. There was no place for him to work: all club owners were afraid to touch him for he was by now controversial *in extremis*; the money was running out; and his heroin habit—another reason he was "dangerous"—was worse than ever.

"Black Lenny Bruce"

On August 3, 1966, Lenny Bruce, just forty, died of an overdose, and was found with a spike sticking out of his right arm.

Fame dies fast. Six years later, a seventeen-year-old comic, a high school dropout named Freddie Prinze was knocking 'em dead at The Improv in New York. And, as he said, "I was *dy-no-mite*. All these managers suddenly wanted me, and one said, 'You are the *first* young comedian to remind me of Lenny Bruce!' *Who?* I did *not* know who the fuck *Lenny Bruce* was! 'You've got to choose,' the manager said, 'choose *now* between being very hip or going very commercial.' "

He chose television, the squeaky-clean *Chico and the Man*, which made him a star overnight, but in his club appearances he would revert and turn the air purple with obscenities. And people kept calling him the "second" Lenny Bruce. By that time, he *knew* who Lenny Bruce was. He even found himself dating Lenny Bruce's daughter, Kitty, who told him, "You are the first comic to make me laugh since my father." He may have been flattered to hear her say it, but the comparison frightened him. "Look," he would say to others, "I do not *want* to sound like Lenny Bruce. I do not want to be *compared* to Lenny Bruce. I do not want to end up like Lenny Bruce."

He did, of course, but he did it differently, with uppers, downers, Quaaludes and, on January 29, 1977, a pistol shot through the head. He was twenty-two.

Freddie Prinze's main man was never Lenny Bruce. It was always, and only, Richard Pryor, his closest friend in Hollywood. He idolized him. Only one photograph was hung on the wall in his living room: Richard Pryor. Never mind that when Prinze was dead Richard Pryor was not permitted to serve as a pall-bearer, was forbidden in fact, by Freddie Prinze's widow even to attend the funeral service. But that is another story.

Comedic influences. A river ever flowing backwards. Prinze to Pryor to Bruce. . . . But who knows whence Lenny Bruce sprang, fullblown with his dirty words and flagellating irreverence that exorcised the devilish repressions of the tribe?

Lenny Bruce, the brash, risk-taking, acid-tongued hipster, subscriber to the theory that the free use of obscenities neutralized and purified them, was a vital influence in Richard Pryor's development and philosophy about comedy. He had been from the time Pryor first heard one of his records, *I Am Not a Nut, Elect Me!*; he was more so after the aspiring comic witnessed him "live" in New York cabarets. From that point, Richard Pryor began to chart his tell-it-like-it-is creative course.

Yet, when Pryor first ventured in the sixties to insert new, outspoken material into his act, he bombed. Nightclub patrons hassled him with shouts of "Not funny" and irate club owners threatened: "Clean up your act or you'll never work here again."

To live, Pryor put his Lenny Bruce "number" on the back burner and, for the next two highly-paid years, did nothing but white bread humor. Until the night of his famous door-closing walkout in 1970 in the midst of a performance at the Aladdin in Vegas.

When he reemerged two years later, a radically changed man, his own angry man, the most ferocious and fiercely funny social critic in all of show business, critics noted his "aura of danger" and "explosive unpredictability." And one of them pinned a label on him that stuck: The Black Ghost of Lenny Bruce.

Just as they had done with Lenny Bruce, Richard Pryor's audiences began to watch, wonder and even worry what he might do next. Some feared that what had happened to Lenny Bruce could happen to Richard Pryor. His rage, wondrous to behold, seemed limitless and somehow alarming. Could he get away with it? To many in his audience, *That Nigger's Crazy* was more than the title on an album cover.

Times had changed since Lenny Bruce. But had they changed enough? The white establishment had brought down Lenny Bruce. Would it let a black comic, a direct descendant of Bruce's school, who also talked "gutter language," and whose fondness for cocaine was as well known as Lenny's for heroin, live? The answer was not long in coming.

History seemed about to repeat itself on August 5, 1974, when, after a performance in Richmond, Virginia, Pryor was arrested on a charge of disorderly conduct for allegedly making obscene remarks on stage.

But the times had changed. Enough.

When that contretemps was over, the comedian would shrug and say, "Oh, that shit. It wasn't nothing. I was doing my act with twelve thousand people there enjoying themselves.

Some white man got offended. They were going to arrest me during the show, but with twelve thousand niggers there enjoying themselves, they had second thoughts."

Unlike Lenny Bruce, who was convicted and jailed for obscenity, the charge against Pryor was dropped two weeks after his arrest, at the request of the prosecution.

Richard Pryor, with all his words, gestures and routines intact, not only lived, *he triumphed,* going on to glories Lenny Bruce had only dreamed about.

Lenny had always sought a wider audience. He desperately wanted his brilliance to be nationally known. It never happened. Only the thousands who bought his records and crowded the clubs in which he appeared knew Lenny Bruce. The rest only knew about him through lurid stories in the tabloids.

Sure, he had his loyal followers among the cognoscenti of the comedic fraternity, but they feared the populace at large wasn't ready for him. Milton Berle urged him to do a clean show. He tried one, on *The Steve Allen Show,* and flopped. Comedy chronicler Lawrence Christon is among those who recall that a very chary Steve Allen introduced Bruce on TV "from across the no man's land of cautious disclaimers."

No other comic prized Lenny Bruce more highly than Bob Hope. Finding himself in the same town as Bruce, he never failed to catch his act.

Bob Hope tells of the time he saw him at the El Patio in Miami: "He came out and he said, 'I understand Bob Hope is in the audience. Where is he?' I sat way in the back and I said, 'I'm here, Lenny.' He said, 'Tonight I'm gonna knock you right on your ass.' And he did. *Wild* material. I fell down, he was so funny. He came running out to the parking lot after the show. He said, 'How about me for your TV program?' And I said, 'Lenny, *you're* good for the educational channel.' "

Lenny Bruce never made it in pictures either, though he'd done a few bits prior to his fame in clubs, and longed to become a movie star. (Ironically, a documentary film made during one of his club performances was posthumously and successfully released in 1968 by Film-Makers Distribution Center. And Dustin Hoffman would later portray him so brilliantly in 1974's *Lenny* that he'd win an Academy Award nomination.)

Richard Pryor now enjoys the huge popularity that Lenny Bruce hungered for. His audience is vast and growing, thanks to the millions of whites added to the great number of devotees among America's twenty-four million blacks (one-third of movie ticket buyers, says *Variety*) who bought his records and flocked to see him in person long before his movie fame.

And now, of course, Pryor not only stars in movies but produces and writes them as well.

Given the opportunity, could Lenny Bruce, canonized figure that he is, ever have made it in movies? It's doubtful, even if he were living now. Going back to that posthumously released film of Bruce doing his stand-up act, you find almost no flexibility in him, even on those rare occasions when he jumps out of his own voice into a character. He appears cocky, self-assured, a sinister spiv who eerily sounds like Dustin Hoffman's Ratso Rizzo in *Midnight Cowboy*. He is clearly not a limitless performer like Pryor.

"I'm everybody, everybody that I can recreate," Richard Pryor said matter-of-factly about his own versatility. "I'm somehow part of them. I've got the same things in me, no matter how terrible they are. Maybe I don't do the same things, but I know. There is no kind of person I can't play. No, not even Hitler, really. Unfortunately."

Asked by reporter Jerry Tallmer if he feels any strong link between himself and Lenny Bruce, Pryor said, "I don't know. Other than that we are kinsmen, as comics. He was a white man telling white people the shit he saw. He was like a traitor to white society."

And is he, Pryor, a traitor too?

"Yeah, I guess so. In that I see society my way, the way he saw it in his way."

Reminded that years ago Lenny Bruce was saying many of the same things Pryor said now on albums and in concert, and went to jail for it, Pryor pointed out this major difference between them: "He was white. He was telling white people about themselves, some dangerous things. It's not the same. Niggers are my audience. I'm not intruding on the white man's thing at all."

What *about* this Black Ghost of Lenny Bruce label? How valid is it? What do others, experts steeped in comedy, feel about it?

Comedian–actor–screenwriter Buck Henry, in discussing Pryor with the authors, says, "Richard's concert is the funniest one-man performance I've heard since Lenny Bruce. But I wouldn't call him the black Lenny Bruce. I don't think he does the same thing. I think it's real superficial, the comparison. Sometimes I was shocked by Lenny, while I was falling on the floor. Part of the reason you fell on the floor was the pressure of the taboos that were being broken. The same thing doesn't apply to

Richard. I'm not shocked by what he does, because I hear the language all the time. I hear it in films, I hear it in plays. We've been hearing it now for twenty years. So what Richard does is doubly original in that the language no longer shocks, is never used gratuitously, and he makes of it something funnier than anyone else can do. Also, he does things about behavior that are constants in all human behavior. His talent lies in being able to use certain truths to make people laugh. And he doesn't preach. At least he hasn't yet. He hasn't used the events of his getting burned, or being in the hospital, or whatever feelings he's had since then as an excuse to preach to us. He's used it as new material for refining and reinventing the dramatic stuff of his life, which he makes funny. Whereas with Lenny, in the last couple of years, one would go to see him and get a three-hour lecture on the shortcomings of American justice, with very little that was funny or interesting."

Siding with Buck Henry on this point is comedy critic Lawrence Christon of the *Los Angeles Times*, who says of Bruce: "Listening to his records or reading his routines, it's clear that while he was able to play off stereotypes and come up with nimble reversals and asides, he wasn't able to integrate his points about morality, religion, racism or the police into his comedy without coming close to hectoring us. Some of the bits are still amusing . . . but . . . he often belabored the point, impervious to the notion that art *shows*, it doesn't tell."

Says Budd Friedman, former owner of The Improv (where Pryor worked early in his career in New York) and now of a club of the same name in Los Angeles, "You *could* say Richard Pryor is the black Lenny Bruce. He could rightly be compared with him in style and language – not that he's imitating Lenny, but in that he's a groundbreaker, a man who has gone out and done things no one else could do. It's true that Pryor doesn't lecture or go into tirades against the Establishment – and Lenny only did it in his later years – but then Richard, despite everything he's gone through with his race, [has] never gone through what Lenny went through with the police. And I can tell you this, going back fourteen to fifteen years ago to when I first met him, Richard was as good then as he is now. That's unusual. It always takes the country a long time to catch up with the pace of The Improv."

"I know Richard very well," says Michael Schultz, who directed the star in both *Greased Lightning* and *Which Way Is Up?* "He's a genius. And he is, as I've thought for a long time, the modern Lenny Bruce, the modern Charlie Chaplin. But I don't like to put him in the light of other comedians because he is, really, *the modern Richard Pryor.* I don't compare Richard to Bruce in his style of language so much as in his willingness just to be totally honest. Daring. And brave as a comedian. He's fearless. It never goes for the faith, a kind of humor that eventually becomes bad humor. The thing, I think, that people love about Richard is that he always hits on material that is on everyone's mind, whether they're black or white. And he has a real open, warm humanity that just captures the people who would love to be upset by him, to hate him. He always finds a way to make them laugh. Richard has gone much further than Lenny Bruce. He's refused to be limited by himself, his environment, and the people around him. Which I think is what eventually did Lenny Bruce in. He got caught up so much in his own act that it eventually destroyed him."

Lena Horne perceives an interesting, major difference in the two comics' styles, even when they are coming at you from the same place. "Lenny," she says, "had great pain, an underlying anger that was so tangible it almost broke your heart to hear him. Richard lets you off the hook now and then. His sense of frustration is funny because it's what happens to all of us, but he doesn't have that real unhappy terrible anger that Lenny Bruce had. Lenny must have been profoundly hurt in some way. I didn't know him very well but I sense so much tragedy, even when I listen to his records. Richard tells it like it is, but then he says, 'Well, man, that's the way it is, you know.'"

"Lenny Bruce kicked open all the doors," says comedian George Carlin. "And he not only dragged some people through them screaming, but he paid most of the price for the rest of us, inspired by that sort of honesty on stage, to walk through those doors. Both he and Richard had similar tools. There are a certain number of tools that go into a comedian's kit: a mind, observation, converting what you see into some kind of ironic or absurd context, then delivering those words—and they must be words that are arresting—with a certain physical ability. Besides your body, you sometimes use voices to help you, or characterizations. And don't forget that Lenny did do characters, in the same way I do, as they underline and punctuate what you're saying. Richard, of course, often will go off into characters for a whole piece. And sometimes as a comedian you're just using the pace or speed of delivery. So Lenny and Richard share a number of these things—similar tools and similar intensity. As for their so-called dirty words, Richard has used his words in the context of life. He uses them talking about the black experience and the white experience, and the things he has experienced, to support his humor. He doesn't use the words as subjects in themselves as I sometimes do. I'll say, 'Hey, look at this, isn't this funny about language? People won't let you say "cocksucker," and yet half the people do it, and the other half want to have it done.' Once I've exposed the hypocrisy about words I'm free to use the words in context also. Richard, however, since he made his change in style, has always used the words in context, in the service of his comedy. Some people ask whether Richard is the cause or effect of today's freedom of expression. As I see it, Richard is the product of his own genes and his own brilliance, his heredity and his environment, and then what he was forced to do about it from within. And it was surely a painful thing for him to get all that poison out. To look for some other reason outside of Richard for the current freedom of expression is to miss the point. He is responsible, largely, mostly, almost completely for all of this. The fact that he functions well at this time is a happy circumstance. The two things went together fine. But it's still Richard. In another era he would maybe not have been nationally known, but he would have been a brilliant person. And he would have found his recognition in a smaller circle. Something else should be noted about Richard. He doesn't lay on guilt. Not even to his white audience. Instead, he improves them. He makes them aware of the bittersweet experience that life is, especially for the underdog. You know, whites are underdogs too, in a very special other way. The white who goes to see Richard and likes what he does, he becomes black by extension. By will. I think what people get from Richard is a ticket to feel that it's all right to be dissatisfied with what white society, the American experience, has laid on them — the things we've been told to feel and believe. Richard gives people permission to feel like that's bullshit, permission to feel black."

Rob Cohen, producer of Pryor's *The Bingo Long Traveling All-Stars and Motor Kings* and *The Wiz*, says, "Early in his movie career Richard was much angrier, much more radical than he is today. And he was ahead of his time. Like Lenny Bruce, he could have gone on and died before he found acceptance, but the culture has grown up and he is now very much in vogue. So it's been a very fortunate thing for him and for everybody. I think, if anything, he's much more brilliant than Lenny Bruce. Lenny Bruce was a pathfinder, a pioneer. But when you listen to his routines today, they fall very flat. I believe that twenty-five years from now, when you listen to Richard Pryor's routines they will still have the same pizazz. Lenny Bruce's greatest strength was that he would talk publicly about things that previously had been considered extremely private. So his long suit was shock value, which is a very short-lived experience. But that was his thing, to stand up on a stage and go: 'fuck, shit, piss, fuck,' you know. That was it. What you saw is what you got. Richard's great value, on the other hand, is not really shock value. His great value is the *truth* that he's talking about. The fact that he will use words like 'fuck' and 'nigger' and 'honky' and 'motherfucker' and 'pussy eater'—all that stuff is definitely secondary to what he's actually talking about. To my mind, Pryor is not a comedian, he is a humorist. His every single move is based on truth, on observation, on the real picture of the human dilemma. Generally his comedy is based on a painful truth, which he then deals with by twisting it around and making it funny. Like that routine he did years ago called 'When Your Woman Leaves You.' It's a hysterical monologue." [It is also a very personal monologue about the time his woman left him. Pryor made it up on the spot one night in 1974 when appearing at Soul Train in San Francisco's North Beach. It begins: "There ain't nothin' like when a bitch leaves you and tells you why. I mean, I'd rather *anything* than that. I mean, just *kill* me, but don't *explain* the shit to me. Yeah, 'cause there ain't a motherfuckin' thing you can say but. . . ."And it proceeds to explore every emotion inherent in such a situation.] "You can hear the man crying inside and it strikes home with every man who's ever been dumped by a girl he likes, or been frustrated by never being able to get the last word with a woman. It is a brilliant, universally human sketch. Richard is an artist, one who continually dips into his own pain and soft spots, weaknesses and feelings, and comes out with a concoction that is at one and the same time communicative, entertaining and enlightening. He is far more brilliant than Lenny Bruce."

"Lenny Bruce was the original man, in the concept that he had freedom of speech," says comedian David Brenner. "He paved the way for the breakthrough. He crossed the line, though, when he attacked the Catholic church. That's when he went overboard, as far as the public was concerned. Then they went after him and, like all those other people who have spoken out, he was crucified. They played it up to the extent that he was overcome by his own weaknesses. There is no real comparison between Lenny and Richard Pryor in style and language, or any way. Richard Pryor fits in at the top. I'm awed by him. There are maybe a half-dozen geniuses in our field: Woody Allen; Jonathan Winters; Mel Brooks; Shecky Green; Cosby, to some degree; and certainly Pryor, an explosive, unpredictable comedic genius.

Draw the line. They're geniuses. The rest of us are comedians. Pryor is something special. An example of his genius is something I saw him do one night at The Improv. He was doing a routine, a funny act. We were screaming. Then he did this other routine about a nine-year-old junkie on a rooftop of Harlem. Wanting to jump. And the priest comes, and the firemen come, and there's this nine-year-old junkie, right? You're laughing and screaming. Then all of a sudden, at the end, he *jumps*. People in the audience were crying. I never saw a comedian turn laughter into tears so quickly. I know I will never forget it. Is Richard Pryor the black Lenny Bruce? No, he's something better. *He's the black Richard Pryor."*

3.

RICHARD FRANKLIN LENNOX THOMAS PRYOR III, according to the records, was born December 1, 1940. That is only partially true. *A* Richard Pryor was born that day, in Peoria, Illinois, a Richard Pryor who stumbled through the early decades of his life desperate to be someone else, anyone else but his own street-smart, angry, volatile self. His earliest hero–role model, as with most American teens before the birth of rock, was a movie star.

"As a kid," Pryor recalled, "I used to live in the movie houses and my idol was Lash LaRue. I wanted to be just like him, I wanted to *be* him." Lash LaRue. A cowboy. Bogart-type. White, of course. Garbed, contrary to tradition, all in black: black boots, black breeches, black shirt, black scarf, black hat, with a mean black whip that cracked down many a villain. And flashy. Though he earned more from the royalties on his comic books than from his grade C movies and lived in furnished flats, he used to tootle around Hollywood in a dazzling blue Cadillac with his signature, "Lash," emblazoned across the door in gold lettering.

Pryor eventually got part of his wish. He played a cowboy very like Lash LaRue – black shirt, black hat – in *Adios Amigo*, a low-budget Western spoof shot in nine days (in 1976) with no redeeming features. "Tell them I apologize," is the final message he sends his fans. "Tell them I needed some money."

But he's fortunate that the Good Lord wasn't listening when he yearned to *be* Lash LaRue, a self-described "triple schizophrenic" who, in his later hard-scrabble years, has had more than his share of run-ins with the law, including, in 1966, an arrest for vagrancy in Miami with just thirty-five cents in his pocket. Of that, Lash LaRue has said, "I walked up to this cop, and he knew who I was, and I knew who he was, and I said, 'Hey, why don't you destroy me, motherfucker? You'd be doing me a favor to put me out of my misery.' He blew his whistle and there were suddenly cops all over me and some big dyke was jabbing me in the ass with a needle."

Later, there was a hard-core porn film, *Hard on the Trail* ("It should've been *Hard-on on the Trail*; just another example of how Hollywood degrades its discarded packages"), and a stint as

Born Twice

a maverick preacher of the gospel, during which, in 1975, LaRue was convicted of possession of marijuana in Jonesboro, Georgia. After testifying "in the name of the Father, the Son and the Holy Ghost" that he was just trying to "save the souls" of two hitch-hikers when he took the marijuana, he was sentenced to twelve months' probation and fined three hundred and fifty dollars. This drug conviction was later overturned by the Georgia Supreme Court which ruled 7–2 that the drugs taken in the search could not be used as evidence.

A while back, a New York editor, wishing to do a "Whatever happened to" piece on Lash LaRue, tracked the former star down to a rooming house on a side street in Hollywood. He received this astonishing letter from Richard Pryor's boyhood idol, scrawled on yellow lined paper:

"I have been preparing all my life for a one night stand and I'm not yet booked.

"In 1963 I became aware I had lived before in another area of time. Kennedy was killed that time in Tampa. This time in Dallas. The same things were happening over again under slight-ly different circumstances. I had lived and died in an area of time estimated to be 10 years ahead of this area. Since we are coming to the time of my demise again it is my desire to share what I know to be true. Between the Masons and the Catholics there is such a confusion you can't die one time and find out which side your [sic] on.

"If the world can't conform you or control you it will kill you and if you don't die when they try–you will be degraded till you would welcome death. That's where I am, in abject poverty waiting the relief of death. If I have to come back again it will be as a black witch doctor speaking no English.

"I am writting [sic] a story, 'The Prophet From Hell,' which may be worth something after I get an acknowledgd [sic] funeral.

"Thank you for your interest. Sincerely, Lash LaRue."

The signature was familiar to the editor. He had seen it before–in gold lettering on that long-ago blue Cadillac.

Clearly, Lash LaRue is a man possessed of his own set of demons, stranger and blacker than those that hilariously burst forth from the comedian's inner storehouse. Could the young Richard Pryor have perceived these demons? Was that part of the cowboy's allure?

As a struggling young comic in New York in the '60s, Richard Pryor did more than aspire to "be" someone else. Lacking any style of his own, he made determined forays into the established territory of other comedians.

For a while, he was Bob Hope, zinging out the topical one-liners, rat-a-tat-tat. He experimented as a younger version of Redd Foxx's wild old curmudgeon. (Red Foxx now says of his once slavish imitator: "I don't care what anyone says, Richard Pryor is the funniest motherfucker around.") He emulated Lenny Bruce's profane attack, a brand of humor he personally admired, lacquering it onto his own black experience, trotting out the word "nigger" for the first time in his act. But the world wasn't ready for that. Audiences heckled him, fellow blacks censured him, clubs banned him with the warning that he "would never work again in the mainstream of the industry if he kept trying to be Supernigger." Rather than starve, he pulled back. Frantic for the right role model, he hit on Bill Cosby, greatly popular in clubs then, and he swallowed him whole. Ask anyone who caught his act at clubs like Cafe Wha? and The Improvisation.

Pryor has recalled watching and studying Cosby, and thinking, "Goddamn it. This nigger's doin' what I'm fixin' to do. I want to be the only nigger. Ain't room for two niggers."

The goad for copying the first black comic who had reached a broad white audience was economic. He imitated Cosby, not because he particularly admired him, but because, he has said, a white agent told him that Cosby was the kind of black man white television viewers would not mind having in their homes.

His career was launched when he began imitating Bill Cosby in the extreme. "I wouldn't admit it, though, but, you know, like Cosby did 'Noah' – I did 'Adam and Eve,' you know what I mean? And like, a comic was set in people's mind, what a comic was. He was a guy who came out and made you laugh. I mean it was that simple."

Pryor's derivative act took him a long way. Soon he was getting national exposure as a guest comic on television: Rudy Vallee's *On Broadway Tonight*; the talk shows of Merv Griffin and Johnny Carson; and, more rewarding than any since its audience was vast and it was for years in Nielsen's Top Ten, *The Ed Sullivan Show*.

Patriotic Pryor, 1976.

Lash LaRue, Pryor's childhood hero.

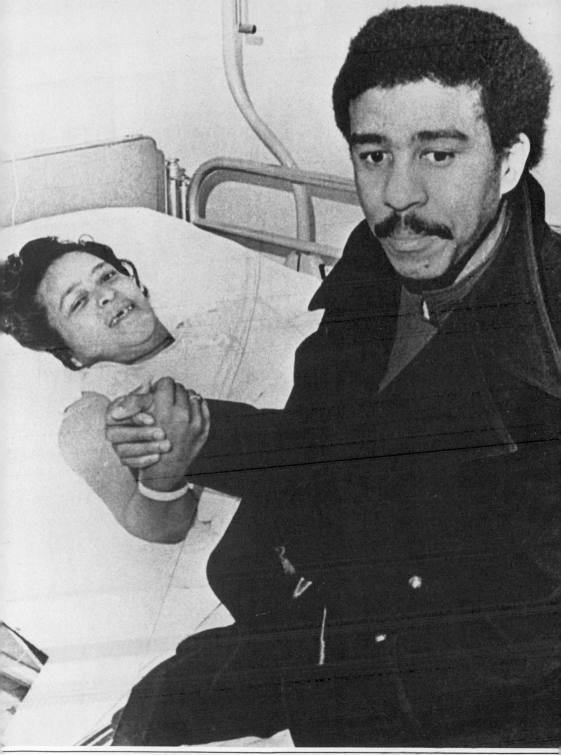

Waiting his turn at bat in 1966 with the Daisy Softball Team, Barrington Playground,
West Los Angeles. Others on the team included Paul Newman and Ryan O'Neal.

Turning his back at a jeering Hollywood Bowl audience during a 1977 fundraiser.

At ''A Tribute to Ali'' on September 6, 1979.

The Divine James L. White's "Religious Telethon," from *The Richard Pryor Special?*

Pryor as "Wino," in a bar-room sketch from
The Richard Pryor Special?, on NBC-TV, May 5, 1977.

Playing Idi Amin Dada in a rebuttal to an NBC editorial, on his *Special*.

Pryor was wearing a flesh-colored body suit, but this
segment was censored from an NBC *Special*.

Bumbling, stumbling Ed Sullivan may not live in everyone's memory as a crusader for black equality in entertainment. Yet he was that, long before it became fashionable. Despite vigorous, and sometimes virulent, industry opposition, he was the first television host to present an integrated show. When his Sunday evening variety show, first titled *Toast of the Town*, made its debut in 1948, Southern representatives of his original sponsor, Emerson Radio, urged Sullivan not to employ black—or Negro, as the expression still was—entertainers, arguing that it would "ruin business." Ed Sullivan stuck by his guns, insisting, "It would be impossible to put on a worthwhile show without availing one's self of Negro talent." Continuing to encounter opposition from nervous sponsors through the years, Sullivan declared, "If the time ever came when I couldn't exercise complete freedom on the talent I'd selected, I'd get the hell off. In booking acts I've never thought in terms of religion or color. I'm looking solely for fine performers who have something on the ball."

Dozens of black performers got their shot—often their first—at national exposure on *The Ed Sullivan Show*: Moms Mabley, Nipsey Russell, Dick Gregory, Pigmeat Markham, George Kirby, Slappy White, Bill Cosby, and, five times in the '60s, the "new" Bill Cosby, Richard Pryor.

Richard Pryor as amiable, ingratiating, "safe" Bill Cosby, however, was not a transformation made in Heaven. At that point in his career, refusing to exploit his color, Cosby would ask, "Why should I go out there and say, 'Ladies and gentlemen, I grew up in a Negro neighborhood?' " (A bit later, in 1969, his color consciousness raised, Cosby attempted to change his image. This was on the TV series *The Bill Cosby Show*, in which black characters resembled familiar people of impeccable normalcy, while the stereotypes moved into the white area. "That's done on purpose," he said then. "If the public can appreciate this, then they will know that changes have come about in what we the black race are doing in contemporary society." The show failed.)

Beyond color, high school dropout Pryor had next to nothing in common with straight-arrow Cosby. With his father in the Navy and generally an absentee parent, Cosby had had to help his mother support and discipline his three younger brothers, and went into show business directly after three years at Temple University in Philadelphia.

Richard Pryor's own background, vastly different, was, as he has so often related, sordid in the extreme.

Consider some of the quotes attributed to him about growing up in the red-light district of the black ghetto of Peoria.

His family operated a string of whorehouses, he has said,

and his paternal grandmother, Marie Pryor Bryant, a New Orleans Creole and Catholic, was the owner. "My grandmother," he said to Ace Burgess in a *Gallery* magazine article, "was the madam. We had three houses on one block – 313, 317, and 324 North Washington. My grandmother was the rule, the power base, a very strong woman."

Elaborating on the setting in which he grew up, Pryor told Barbara Walters in a television interview, "China Bee was next door. That was a magic place, right? And then down the street was Joe Eagle. Was an Italian dude. He had the only white whorehouse on the block. And he got a different clientele, and the women got paid more. And we hated them. You want to know?

"All right, now, it was like about ten houses along this block, Washington Street. And every house had a different law. You know, you had to be different. And those were in the days when the women used to peck on the window with quarters – t-t-t-t-t for people. Customers. T-t-t. 'Hello. Hey, sweetie, baby.' They'd be talking through the window. And nobody could hear them out in the streets, right."

And one of those women tapping on the window and turning tricks with drunken whites, or any other man with the folding money, he has repeatedly said, was his own mother, Gertrude Thomas Pryor, the wife of Marie Bryant's son Leroy "Buck." ("They got married when I was about three," said Pryor.)

The comedian's ghetto memories of Peoria – if not his family experiences there – are corroborated by television newscaster Sander Vanocur, who also grew up in this tough industrial Illinois town.

"North Washington Street," says Vanocur, "was noted for its string of whorehouses in those days, and they began right after my uncle's produce house on North Washington. There were three establishments catering to the white trade, then a cross street, and the next block was filled with establishments catering to the black clientele."

To Barbara Walters, Pryor noted of his childhood, "It was hell, because I had nobody to talk to. I was a child, right, and I grew up seeing my mother going to rooms with men, and my aunties going to rooms with men, you understand? And I saw no man in charge. Now I used to peek through keyholes and watch people make love, not love . . . but to me it was love. It hasn't messed me up but I'll say it messed me up sexually. . . ."

Continuing, Pryor declared that he was fourteen when his first child, a daughter, was born. (Actually, in an interview printed in late 1976, he stated that Renee would "be 20 in April." April 1977. Meaning she was born when he was really sixteen. No matter, her birth is sufficient proof that Richard Pryor, as he has said, "was fucking early.")

Her mother – no name given – was presumably a young girl he had "in the garage."

"I didn't know my father was making love to her, too," he told Barbara Walters. "That's the truth. I went home to my father, when she told me she was pregnant, and I cried. I was standing in the dining room. I was crying. My mother said, 'What's wrong with you, boy?' Father says, 'There ain't nothing wrong with him, he got some girl pregnant.' And I started crying real big, you know, and he said, 'Oh, serious?' And he took me in the front room and he talked to me about it and he told me that he'd had her . . . made love to her. You know . . . I thought she'd never made love to nobody. . . ."

By the age he was then, fourteen or sixteen, Richard Pryor was already a high school dropout, already had a checkered past in Peoria, and had already given evidence that he was a survivor.

Some of the credit for the last, he said, goes to his mother.

"My mother went through a lot of hell behind me," he observed, "because people would tell her, 'You don't take care of that boy.' She always wanted me to be somebody and she wasn't the strongest person in the world. But I give her a lot of credit. At least she didn't flush me down the toilet like some do. I'm not trying to be crude but I found a baby in a shoe box once when I was a kid – dead."

Even though he has claimed to have seen "my father fighting my mother," he recalled of both his parents, and those early times, "it was hard. They did the best they could. They taught me stuff that the average person doesn't get to learn, like real morals and honesty and dignity. You have to have that if you're going to live in the streets. Your word is all you have. That's the most important thing I learned."

But, there is no denying, his early years were hard – and nothing changed for longer than he likes to remember.

His education was erratic. Reportedly, he was expelled from a Catholic school when nuns discovered what his family did for a living. "I didn't care so much for me," he said, "but it made my mother cry." Could such a secret have been kept for long, though, in wide-open Peoria? At any rate, he was transferred to a public school. There, because of his hyperactivity, he was put into a class for the mentally retarded. He was black, verbal, noisy, a prankster who had discovered that he could attract attention by emitting fierce Tarzan yells (not always choosing the right time or place to do so), and he would not conform to the regimentation of the classroom. "I wasn't able to express myself," he said. "Instead, I would demonstrate it in some way, like playing hooky from school, or acting up in class." He remained in classes for slow learners until he was expelled in the seventh grade – permanently – for hitting a male science teacher in the face.

"I wasn't tough as a kid, no," he once insisted to *Washington Post* correspondent Henry Allen. "I hung around with a lot of tough guys, but you see, I wasn't afraid like they were afraid. You follow me? You say it's like my nerve endings are on top of my skin. Right. That's my tool, my temper. I wouldn't want to cover it up, to protect myself because then I'd lose something."

The young Richard Pryor already had another secret weapon, besides lack of fear, in his arsenal of weapons – his humor.

A Peoria family friend told a *Playboy* reporter, "At that time, he did comedy in self-defense. He was small and to keep kids from beating on him, he cracked them up. I remember a family named Clark always pushed people around, but not Richard. Because he kept them laughing."

To survive, he took menial jobs. He was a janitor for a while, a truckdriver, and a packing-house laborer. He considered being a prizefighter, slight of build though he was. After winning his first fight in the first round in a Golden Gloves tournament, he had second thoughts about this occupation, "I think he did it by telling a joke, which made the guy double up. And then he punched him out." Also, the comic has added, there was a period when he indulged in petty thievery. "We used to go till-tapping and I always got caught," he said. "My father kicked ass all the way up Washington Street."

And at least once he saw the inside of a Peoria jail. According to reporter William Brashler, he became embroiled in a fight involving "two neighborhood gangs called the Love Licks and the Love Veedles. He and a dozen others were arrested, relieved of knives and rubber hoses and locked up."

Describing being roughed up in jail by the cops, Pryor demonstrated how it was. He crossed his arm in front of his neck to show how the policemen held him. Then slowly, deliberately, he thrust the other hand forward to show how the cops punched him in the kidney.

"I decided that I was not the motherfucker who was going to get hit in the kidney again. That bothered me a lot. But killers always understand why you don't want to get hurt. It's the others, *they* get you into trouble. Killers, they *survive*."

To survive, if not to learn to be a killer, but to put trouble behind him, at least temporarily, he enlisted in the Army at age seventeen. Patriotism did not enter into his decision, he explained. "It was something to do, man. It was a way to get out of Peoria."

His escape from Peoria took him to France and Germany. It was only a two-year respite, and is not recalled as a halcyon time in his life. He found racism just as rampant in the peacetime service as he had back home, and he got into trouble.

"I did hit a cat in the head with a pipe," he confessed. "You know why? Those three white boys had me cornered in an armory, in a tank division, and they were beating me with tire irons, and I found a pipe, and I hit one of them in the head—a cracker." Then he added, laughing, "And he said, 'Well, damn! You're all right with me, I'll tell you that.' "

While he did have a chance to entertain in a few camp shows, the Army mainly kept him otherwise occupied.

"I tell everybody that I was a paratrooper, but I was a plumber," he said. "I took an IQ test. They looked at it and said, 'This nigger's too dumb. Let's send him to plumbing school.' And they did."

Back home in Peoria at nineteen, with an honorable discharge, Pryor got married. Or so it has been said. But he and his wife—or mate—parted soon after the birth of a son, Richard Jr.

In his old neighborhood on North Washington Street, he began performing as a comedian at Collins Corner. The club's proprietor, Bris Collins, considered the most powerful black in Peoria, paid him what Pryor considered a princely sum—seventy-two dollars a week.

But he shortly left Peoria for good because, he maintains, his father threw him out of the house.

As Pryor later explained to Sander Vanocur, "I was going to be a pimp. And my father took my whore from me. He told me that I didn't need her, that I really hadn't understood her. And I *didn't* understand her. This woman gave me money and told me to beat her. So she hit me and I started fighting—for my life. I had no idea what she was talking about. I went berserk. I didn't know there was any romantic connotation to physical violence."

Apparently he has since learned. Not long ago he said he wanted to co-star with blonde Cybill Shepherd in a remake of Lina Wertmuller's *Swept Away*, in which a snooty bourgeois beauty gets marooned on an island and slapped around by a dark macho man whom she eventually begs to ravish her. "I liked it because it's cruel, and that's sexy," he said.

Yet it was from his father, who kicked him out of the house, as Pryor once told Ace Burgess, that he learned the most as a comedian.

"He was seriously funny," Pryor said, "and he'd say things that would blow your mind. When my mother died, he went to the funeral and it was about fourteen below zero. My dad was sitting in the car and he was crying, and as he was crying, he says, 'If it gets any colder they'll have to bury the bitch by herself.' . . . And everybody started laughing in the car. When we were out by the grave and the preacher was talking, my Pop says, 'Cut the shit, man, hurry up! It's fourteen below out here.' Dad was fun. He had a lot of heart. That's where I get most of my humor, from people with heart that stand up for what they are. They're real, they don't have false feelings, they say what they mean."

Leaving Peoria, Richard Pryor took his comedy on the road, playing every club open to young black comedians in the U.S. and Canada. Cribbing his material from joke books, he did stints in East St. Louis (appearing alongside a troupe of female impersonators), Buffalo, Windsor (sharing the stage with an act featuring a wrestling bear prone to heavy tippling), Detroit, and Toronto. There he stayed at a hotel favored, he soon realized, by gay wrestlers. "They were huge, big fags. I couldn't believe it. I mean, you'd see them brutally murdering each other in Saturday night wrestling matches. And then you'd see them back at the hotel, kissing and holding hands. It was bizarre." His "education" continued at the Zanzibar in Youngstown, Ohio: "Arabs owned it. I had to pull a blank pistol on the cat to get my money."

Then there was Pittsburgh where he encountered his first serious trouble with the police. A girlfriend brought assault and battery charges against him and he landed in the clink for thirty-five days. "It was a valid charge," he confessed. "We had this misunderstanding. I really assaulted her and I really battered her."

Sharing his cell was an older man who had once been a boyfriend of one of Pryor's aunts in Peoria. Since the young comedian was too proud to ask his folks for help, the man took it upon himself to notify his old girlfriend of her nephew's present plight. She immediately wired the money he needed to get to New York when he was released.

After paying bus fare and buying a new suit, Richard Pryor arrived in New York in 1963 with something like two dollars in his pocket. He headed for Greenwich Village, to the little clubs, where as a stand-up comic he was soon earning the grandiose sum of five dollars a night. He went through his trial-and-error periods – as Bob Hope, Redd Foxx, Pigmeat Markham, Dick Gregory – as, even, a young male version of shuffling Moms Mabley. Then he discovered the "perfect" model, on the tail of whose comedy comet he could, he was sure, breeze through to the bigtime – Bill Cosby.

What could have possessed him? What could have made him believe that their individual black experiences – as distant from one another as the millions of light years separating earth and the nearest quasar – could ever be shaped into the same pattern?

Interestingly enough, however, they did have one thing in common – similar floundering beginnings as comedians.

Like Pryor, Bill Cosby had difficulty finding his footing as a comedian. Groping for a style and having no material of his own, he had no qualms about borrowing from already arrived comics like Mel Brooks, Carl Reiner, and, yes, Lenny Bruce, too. He even attempted racial humor in the Dick Gregory vein, but shucked it when he realized it was not his bag.

Soon Bill Cosby discovered that jokes were not his thing, either. His forte was swinging homespun philosophy. Projecting the combined image of a groovy Mark Twain and a hip Harry Golden who drew no sharp line between autobiography and invention, he clicked.

This, then, was the suit that Richard Pryor appropriated. It didn't fit his frame but he kept wearing it. He found acceptance in it. He wore it on the TV shows of Ed Sullivan, Steve Allen and Merv Griffin. And, constricting as it was, it damn near killed him.

"In his early days there was a lot of Bill Cosby in Richard's act," admits Bill Cosby. "Then one evening I was in the audience when Richard took on a whole new persona – his own. In front of me and everyone else, Richard killed the Bill Cosby in his act, made people hate it. Then he worked on them, doing pure Richard Pryor, and it was the most astonishing metamorphosis I have ever seen. He was magnificent."

It was not to be a lasting switch-over, though. Not yet. To stay alive, he had to go back to being an approximation of Bill Cosby. "White bread" humor was fine for Cosby but not for him, and he knew it.

"Yeah, I used to do Cosby's material and it was unnatural," Pryor has admitted. " 'Good evening, ladies and gentlemen, ha, ha. You know, a funny thing happened, hee, hee,' . . . It really wasn't me."

There were characters in his head kicking, screaming,

and cursing to be set free: characters, or reasonable facsimiles thereof, from his raunchy growing-up years on North Washington Street in Peoria. Big Black Bertha, "the 300-pound woman with a 280-pound ass." Prostitutes. Pimps. Numbers runners. Prison wardens. Rogues. Judges. Oilwell, the "dangerous nigger," the macho braggart proclaiming, "I'm Oil*wellll*, 6-foot-5, 222 pounds of *mannn*," who fights the cops. The junkie who tells an officious bureaucrat who has just read his police record: "I know I'm a criminal. Why don't you tell me something I don't know – like where I'm going to find a job." Silver-sequined Rev. James L. White in his silver boots, contemptuous of little black dollars from little black people, who declares, "We're looking for the Billy Graham dollars." Mudbone, the ancient levee-tender "who used to dip snuff and sit in front of the store and spit, that was his job." The Wino dealing with Dracula ("Say, nigger, you with the cape. What you doin' peekin' in them people's window? What's your name, boy? Dracula? What kind of name is that for a nigger? Where you from, fool? Transylvania? I know where it is, nigger. You ain't the smartest motherfucker in the world, even though you is the ugliest. . . . Why don't you get your teeth fixed, nigger – that ugly shit hanging all out of your mouth.")

On a night in Las Vegas in 1970, the characters had their way. They forced the man whose seething imagination sired them to surrender and he ceased peddling artificial secondhand crap.

"It wasn't me," Pryor later explained to *Rolling Stone* writer David Felton. "The current was happening, and every now and then I'd go for it. And people would tell me, 'You can't do that.' If I said 'ass' or something, they'd say, 'Hey, you can't have that in there.' And I'd think, 'Why in the fuck? . . . *Fuck* these people, man, *fuck* this way of livin', *fuck* it.' "

In the middle of his act at the Aladdin Hotel, Pryor stopped, looked out at his mostly white audience, and said, "What the fuck am I doing here?" Then he walked off the stage. His old life was over.

Richard Pryor, *the* Richard Pryor, was not born, miraculously, that evening. But birth pains, so severe and traumatic that he later termed them "a walking nervous breakdown," had set in. They were accompanied by widely circulated rumors that he would never work again, certainly not in the big time.

For two years, he holed up in a cheap apartment in Berkeley, California. He worked on his characters, trying out his abrasive new comedy style (when he felt like it) on hippies in little clubs around San Francisco. He worked for peanuts, but he was happy, he said, because "I felt free, like I had just come out of a dungeon I had been in for years."

He bought a Marvin Gaye record, *What's Going On,* and played it over and over until it wore out. He accumulated debts of six hundred thousand dollars, much of it for cocaine, then a hundred dollar-a-day habit. ("I snorted up Peru. I could have *bought* Peru.")

And, more crucial than anything else to his eventual re-emergence as a drastically changed man and entertainer, he said, "I read some of Malcolm X's speeches and thought, hey, there's someone who thinks like I do. I'm not crazy."

He read on. And the old Richard Pryor, who craved acceptance, and would do anything to win the world's loving approval, disappeared. No one would ever see him again.

4.

MALCOLM X WAS, OF COURSE, THREE VERY different men in his thirty-nine-year life. Until 1952, he was Malcolm Little, a railroad dining-car steward, pimp, bootlegger, dope peddler, and ex-con. That year, at age twenty-six, he fell under the powerful influence of Elijah Muhammad, head of the Black Muslims, and, giving up his "slave name," became Malcolm X. No Muslim ever believed or preached more ferociously that the white man is the "devil," and that the black is superior to the white in all ways – morally, spiritually, and intellectually. Malcolm X rose quickly to dizzying heights of fame and power. Not only was he Muhammad's business manager and prime minister, but it was widely believed that he would be Muhammad's successor as well. Angered and feeling threatened, the older leader expelled Malcolm X from the Black Muslims in 1963. The following year, after a pilgrimage to Africa and the Muslim Holy Cities, Malcolm X converted to Mohammedanism. Changing his name once more, to El-Hajj Malik El-Shabazz, he founded the Organization of Afro-American Unity. His new organization was described as "a non-religious and non-sectarian group organized to unite Afro-Americans for a constructive program toward attainment of human rights." The former Malcolm X also softened his attitude toward whites. He was now opposed to radical racism, he maintained. Instead, he believed that whites were "human beings as long as this is borne out by their humane attitude toward Negroes." Rivalry between his OAAU and the Black Muslims was fierce. He died a violent shotgun death at an OAAU meeting near Harlem on February 21, 1965. Convicted of his murder and sentenced to life imprisonment were an avowed Muslim and two alleged Black Muslims.

Which Malcolm X evoked a feeling of brotherhood and kinship in Richard Pryor during his agonized months of retreat and inner searching in Berkeley?

Certainly it was not Malcolm Little. Possibly it was not El-Hajj Malik El-Shabazz, either. Surely it was the one in the middle, the Malcolm X with the strident, dogmatic views on racism and the white man. Richard Pryor could never become a Black Muslim – not with its compulsory oath to abstain forever

Malcolm X and Whitey

from drinking, smoking, cursing, gambling, dancing and sexual promiscuity. No way. But, as for listening to Malcolm X's teachings about blacks and whites, perhaps that was something else again.

Said Malcolm X in a *Playboy* interview with *Roots* author Alex Haley in 1963: "The white man has taught the black people in this country to hate themselves as inferior, to hate each other, to be divided against each other.

"The brainwashed black man can never learn to stand on his own two feet until he is on his own. We must learn to become our own producers, manufacturers and traders; we must have industry of our own, to employ our own. The white man . . . wants to keep the black man always dependent and begging . . . where he can be watched and retarded.

"The black man is a whole lot smarter than white people think he is. The black man has survived in this country by fooling the white man. He's been dancing and grinning and white men never guessed what he was thinking.

"Allah is going to wake up all black men to see the white man as he really is. . . .

"The black masses are learning for the first time in 400 years the real truth of how the white man brainwashed the black man, kept him ignorant of his true history, robbed him of his self-confidence. . . .

"I've never seen a sincere white man, not when it comes to helping black people. . . . The white man is interested in the black man only to the extent that the black man is of use to him. The white man's interest is to make money, to exploit. . . .

"White society has always considered that one drop of black blood makes you black. To me, if one drop can do this, it only shows the power of one drop of black blood. . . .

"Any white man is against blacks. The entire American economy is based on white supremacy. . . .

"The world since Adam has been white – and corrupt. The world of tomorrow will be black – and righteous. . . . In the black world of tomorrow, there will be *true* freedom, justice and equality for all."

Something somewhere in this stirred Richard Pryor's long dormant feelings. He *was* black. He was *proud* to be black. He *felt* for the blacks, he suffered their pain. He *loved* black people. And the other thing that he loved – his work, his comedy – would henceforth be *all-black*, though satirizing blacks as well as whites. If whites laughed too, well, it was allowed. If not, no matter. From that moment forward, in Pryor's scheme of things whites were relegated to the back of the bus.

In 1972, the new, the reconstructed Richard Pryor came out of the closet.

He took his revolutionary new material not to Las Vegas, or any of the fancier night spots in Manhattan, but to Harlem, to the Apollo, the legendary theater now closed, whose audiences have seen and passed judgment on every black entertainer in history. And he confessed, "I was scared to death. Them niggers will eat you up if your shit ain't right. But they responded and I was fine after that, wherever I went. I worked Detroit, Chicago – every place the same. People felt good. And to see people laughing at each other and not being so serious, that made me feel good."

His revised act was a total departure from anything he'd ever done before. In it, he turned for inspiration to the street people and the real-life situations that he knew better than any comic alive. For the first time his characters, who almost drove him mad when he denied them, *lived.*

He recorded a new album, only his second: *Craps, After Hours.* With language that singed the ears and its funky characters, it was light years away from his first, simply titled *Richard Pryor.* Of that vinyl debut, issued in 1968, critic David Felton says, "The album is interesting to go back to and hear since it includes the sort of material he seldom does any more. His characters are as well acted as today, but the situations tend to be more traditional and contrived – a TV panel show, a Superman parody, a prison play. Yet his contrivances are extremely imaginative, and because they are less down-to-earth than the street action he performs today, they reveal a sense of nonsense and fantasy that he now mainly reserves for private displays." *Craps, After Hours* was something else. On it, just as in his "live" act, was *the* Richard Pryor – fiercely, shockingly, hilariously black; abrasive, hostile, anti-establishment, cynical, realistic, dirty-mouthed, irreverent, outrageous, obscene, angry, mischievous, coarse, controversial. His was the raw, fresh, vibrant humor of the black experience in America. Almost universally, critics agreed that by transforming his "anger and resentment into devastatingly effective humor," Richard Pryor had emerged as the funniest man, white or black, alive.

Not missing from his turn-around album was Pryor's operative word, by now almost patented, once considered the most hateful epithet in the black community: "nigger."

But, as *Time* magazine later observed, "When Richard Pryor says it, it means something different from what it did through too much of America's history. Depending on his inflection or even the tilt of his mouth, it can mean simply black. Or it can mean a hip black, wise in the ways of the street. Occasionally, nigger can even mean white in Pryor's reverse English lexicon. However he defines it, Pryor is certain of one thing. He is proudly, assertively a nigger, the first comedian to speak in the raw, brutal, but often wildly hilarious language of the streets."

Along with bringing his act "back in spirit to Peoria's black ghetto and the mean streets all over the U.S.," continued the *Time* critic, "he started to talk in the argot of the pool shark and the hustler, a language so obscene that it is no longer obscene, with four-letter words so common that they now seem part of the verbal furniture."

His street-wise, cut-to-the-marrow style – characterized by critic Henry Allen as "that scorching roar of obscene and racial invective . . . material that dredges up all our worst fears and leaves us cringing with laughter" – became even more *outré* in the albums that followed *Craps, After Hours.*

Since 1974, recording extensively for Warners/Reprise, Pryor has had five salty-language monster successes: *That Nigger's Crazy* (a certified Gold and Platinum hit which won him a Grammy plus both the NATRA Award for Comedian of the Year and *Record World's* Comedy Album of the Year honor), *Is It Something I Said?* (another Grammy), *Bicentennial Nigger* (said *Variety:* "Richard Pryor, a comic who consistently has hits on disc despite material not suited for airplay, has another uproarious program"), *Greatest Hits* and *Wanted: Richard Pryor.*

It is the growth in the artist, not only on records but even more so in concert performances (since he is visually the most expressive comic since Chaplin) that has caused his audience to swell to gargantuan proportions.

Writer James McPherson perceptively observed that "he enters into his people and allows whatever is comic in them, whatever is human, to evolve out of what they say and how they look into a total scene. It is part of Richard Pryor's genius that, through the selective use of facial expressions, gestures, emphases in speech and movements, he can create a scene that is comic and at the same time recognizable as profoundly human."

"Genius" is a key word in the above passage. Its usage has by now become obligatory in Pryor reviews.

And a *Rolling Stone* critic provided the proper frame of reference for Richard Pryor's comedy style by labeling it "a new type of realistic theater," a theater presenting "the blemished, the pretentious, the lame—the common affairs and crutches of common people."

Racism is never far from the surface in Richard Pryor's comedy, never so virulent as the Malcolm X brand, but there nonetheless. And he makes no apology for it.

His family had managed, somehow, to shield him from it until he entered grade school—an integrated school—in Peoria. He quickly learned about racism there in an incident that remains vivid in his memory to this day.

"When I was a little boy," he has said, "I was in love with this little girl in my class, and I brought her a scratch board. You know, one of those gray cardboard things you draw on, and then you lift up the plastic and the picture's gone? The next day, her daddy comes to school and says, 'Don't you dare give my little girl a present.' When I told my father, he just shook his head. You see, nobody had told me about racism, but he knew."

As a result of this and later events, particularly those involving white cops, he holds no particular affection for many whites. So, in his variegated projects as movie actor, concert star and recording artist, he surrounds himself with as many blacks as possible—lawyers, agents, managers, producers, writers, actors, directors.

"He is a man torn between his resentment of being black—and what it means to be black in this country—and his desire to be big, the biggest, in a white-oriented, white-run industry," notes one astute observer.

In Pauline Kael's opinion, "Pryor's comedy isn't based on suspiciousness about whites, or on anger, either; he's gone way past that. Whites are *unbelievable* to him."

In truth, the comic has never said he hates whites. He doesn't; he hates no one, at least not in groups. His barbed humor would be bitter, would not be funny, if he did hate whites. Still he chooses to distance himself from Whitey. With reason. As he said on his Grammy-winning *Bicentennial Nigger* album: "We're celebratin' two hundred years of white folks kicking ass. . . . You all probably have forgotten about it. Well, I ain't never gonna forget it."

Whites, he said, "don't care if we [blacks] wake up or not."
In American courts, he continued, "they give niggers time as if
they were giving lunch. You go looking for justice, and that's just
what you find – just us."

His disdain for whites extends from certain fellow
comedians such as Mel Brooks to presidents (LBJ to Nixon to
Ford to Carter to Reagan) to royalty, like the English princess
who asked him a question at the London premiere of *Silver
Streak* but didn't wait to hear the answer. "I could have hit that
bitch with a brick," he said.

In his opinion, whites have a "tremendous inferiority
complex about themselves when it comes to people with color. It's
like they had been raised and trained in some kind of weird ship.
They come on like they are superior but they're really inferior."

"The time for being white is over," he told another reporter. "I don't have any use for the people that never let you forget what color they are."

White audiences can take him or leave him, Pryor has
declared. "I'm not interested in trying to change my shit to please
white people. I'm not interested in diluting my conversation,
diluting my feelings to please them. They don't try to do nothing
for us. . . . I'm not interested in wasting my life compromising."

When asked – by Ace Burgess – if whites and blacks will
ever be able to live in harmony, he replied, "Can they sing in harmony? I don't really see how. Everything we learn in school is
about white people. They don't want to learn about our ways, so
we can't live in harmony until they learn about us and know who
we are and respect us."

He was at his angriest on *The Tonight Show* in 1978 when
he turned to the audience and said: "If you want to do anything, if
you're black and still here in America, get a gun and go to South
Africa and kill some white people." He had just returned from a
pilgrimage to South Africa and had been shocked by what he had
seen there.

Though once a regular and popular guest on television
talk shows, all of them hosted by whites, Pryor proclaimed he
will not appear on them again. There always comes a time, he explained, "when the host on the talk show turns to you and says,
'Isn't America great, Richard?' and you're supposed to say, 'It
sure is,' and then he says, 'See, guys, *he* did it – what's the matter
with the rest of you?' I've gone along with that in the past,
but no more."

But in truth, despite all, Richard Pryor does think America is great. The evidence is this affirmative quote, given to *Gallery*, when asked his opinion of America: "It's a beautiful country . . . all in all, I still enjoy living in America. It's confusing. On the one hand, there's the rich and on the other you have poverty. It would be all right if it was because of the people, but it's the system. So it's a miracle country, America the beautiful, if you buy that ticket . . . if you can afford to buy it. But I do believe that I couldn't have done what I've done in any other country."

Understandably, it is black America that he loves best. Reminded that he has a vast hip young white public, Pryor shrugged and said of his black audience, "That's all I'm interested in. They're the only ones that have been where I've been, that know what I'm talking about."

Ebony writer Louie Robinson says, "Pryor's humor is obviously out of the joy and pain of his own life and the lives of others he has seen. Consequently, he says, when he starts to develop a comedy routine it often runs to the heavier emotional side before he can turn it into humor. . . . It is that quality of looking into what people – black people – are really feeling that gives Pryor his comic genius. And it is his love for them that gives him the ability to see so deeply."

Pryor on black people: "You look at them – some Brothers and Sisters who can't read, some who may have their combs sticking in their heads, or a big fat black woman with her hair going every which-way – but when you live with them and hear them talk, you know that they are some of the smartest people on the planet because they know stuff that people out at those institutes at Yale and Harvard are trying to get. . . . You come up . . . and you hold on to [your own character] and try to have your principles about you, and you learn all their [whites'] stuff and hold yours and you're a proud black person walking the street. It's amazing! It knocks me out! It makes me cry."

Why is black comedy, particularly his, so rich in subtle shadings and complexities? Pryor's answer: "Niggers just have a way of telling you stuff and not telling you stuff. Martians would have a difficult time with niggers. They be translating words, saying a whole lot of things underneath you, all around you. That's our comedy."

However popular he may become with white audiences – and he is increasingly so because of his movies – Richard Pryor will never forget where he's coming from. Or going. His heart loyally remains with the blacks of the world.

"I often have this dream," he said. "I'm in a beautiful grassy field surrounded by beautiful people and in the middle is an airplane. It's going to heaven, taking all the people there. I'm there too and I begin to look around and realize all the people are very pretty but they're white. So I decide, I don't want to go to heaven if there's not gonna be no niggers there."

On a less esoteric level, he remarked, "If they took all my money away, I'd have to go to some ghetto to live. It ain't gon' be some white neighborhood — I'd have to go live with my people. As long as they like what I do, I know I'm doing all right."

Loving blacks, and verbally flailing the white establishment as he righteously and consistently does, he stops short of hatred for the white man.

James McPherson, after spending time with Pryor for a *New York Times Magazine* profile, offers this telling vignette:

"On the early evening news, there is a feature about Los Angeles people who visit homes for retarded children and the elderly. A mentally retarded white girl is on camera. 'How do you hate that?' he asks. ''Cause she's white? You wish that on her?' A little black boy is bouncing a basketball to entertain a group of elderly white people. 'Look at them old people,' he says, 'that old man sitting up there.' The old man is smiling. The little black boy is smiling. 'How do you have that? 'Cause it's black? I wouldn't want to be like that. Can you imagine the hearts of people all tied up in hatred?' "

Asked pointedly once if he sees everything in terms of black people and white people, Pryor replied, "No. Here's what I see people as. I see people as the nucleus of a great idea that hasn't come to be yet."

5.

"WHEN I WAS A KID, I ALWAYS SAID I WOULD BE in the movies one day," recalled Richard Pryor, and damned if I didn't make it. Sometimes I just sit home and look out the window and say, 'Daaaaammmmm!'"

Indeed he has made it as a movie star, bona fide, bankable, certified gold variety; his presence in a film is worth more to an exhibitor than that of any holder of Hollywood's gold-plated Oscar. His *Stir Crazy*, co-starring Gene Wilder, has gone over the $100-million mark at the box-office. That puts it behind only *Close Encounters of the Third Kind* (more than $116 million) and *Kramer vs. Kramer* (almost $105 million) among Columbia Pictures' three top-grossing films of all time.

In 1972, the pivotal year when everything changed for Richard Pryor, Diana Ross' *Lady Sings the Blues* provided him with the attention-getting supporting role of Billie Holiday's drug-fond Piano Man. "Berry Gordy, who was producing the movie, came up and said, 'I need somebody to do a little comedy,'" Pryor said. Slight pause for dramatic effect. "Then John Wayne died and I took over."

Not all the reviewers were enchanted by his performance. *Films in Review's* critic took him to task for swallowing his lines. Donald Bogle wrote with restraint in his history of blacks in American films, *Toms, Coons, Mulattoes, Mammies & Bucks*, "Richard Pryor proved delightful (although occasionally uncontrollable) as the good-humored piano player." But more critics went along with Howard Kissell of *Women's Wear Daily*, who noted, "There is a show-stealing performance by Richard Pryor as Billie Holiday's pianist, the man who 'discovers' her, helps her throughout her career and, unwittingly, leads her to a crucial breakdown."

It matters little that the reviews on *Lady Sings the Blues* were mixed. Richard Pryor was off and running to become almost singlehandedly Hollywood's black film industry.

All recent "official" studio biographies refer to *Lady Sings the Blues* as the comic's screen debut. Such is not the case. Before it, dating from 1967, he had already played minor roles, garnering small attention, in five films and, in a sixth, was fleet-

Movie-e-e Star

ingly seen doing a snippet from his club act in the oddly titled *Dynamite Chicken*. This was an anti-Vietnam War grab bag featuring film clips (of Lenny Bruce and others), "real" people (Andy Warhol, poet Allen Ginsberg, The Black Panther Party, etc.) and entertainers (John Lennon, Joan Baez, Pryor and others).

Richard Pryor's first small movie role, that of a cop, was in Sid Caesar's *The Busy Body,* a labored mystery farce involving gangsters and corpses. "Supporting comics (including Pryor and Godfrey Cambridge) give the film its funniest moments," said reviewer Leonard Maltin. Another critic wrote, "The young Richard Pryor is too young, but amusing as a police lieutenant."

In Christopher Jones' *Wild in the Streets,* a drama about the explosive movement of the young to lower the voting age to fourteen and take over the U.S. government, Pryor was Stanley X, a drummer. Next was John Wayne's *Green Berets,* in which he played a G.I. Pryor was far down the cast list (#16), and was billed, for some unknown reason, as Richard "Cactus" Pryor. This was followed by *The Phynx,* an all-star abomination, purportedly a farce, which sank without a trace. *You've Got to Walk It Like You Talk It or You'll Lose That Beat,* made in 1971, when he had indeed lost his old beat and was searching for a new one, was the last of Richard Pryor's "unknown" screen appearances.

Wattstax, a film released shortly after *Lady Sings the Blues,* is noteworthy for being the movie in which an assortment of Pryor's characters—yet to become nationally famous—were introduced to theater audiences.

Filmed at the outdoor Watts Summer Festival, August 1972, *Wattstax* interweaves acts by various stars who recorded on the Stax label with street life in the Los Angeles black ghetto of Watts.

Hollywood reporter Les Payne, who had never seen Pryor before, was among those who saw *Wattstax* at its opening, and he exulted, "Richard Pryor is a comic genius without peer in this humorless age." Years later, Payne still vividly recalled the details of the film and the qualities that endeared the comedian to him forever. "Between songs," he said, "the film cut to the scenes of Watts – to a church, to a barbershop, and to Richard Pryor, sitting on a stool in a local bar. Pryor's wildly-dancing eyes and rubbery face – moving from fear, to dread, to joy – played out a genuine and painfully funny account of street life in black America. One moment he was a minister dealing on a personal level with God. Then he was a frightened kid on a mean back street, then a pimp, a wino and a street-wise junkie. Pryor is not truly a stand-up comic. He is a master of improvisation and mime, and he has a rare aural memory that enables him to impersonate anyone. He has mastered a host of characters."

Throughout 1973–74, Richard Pryor, still rebuilding his life and career, remained a supporting actor in films. He supported Billy Dee Williams, one of his close friends, in *Hit!*, playing a private eye. In this gritty drama, Williams was a U.S. agent seeking personal revenge on a top drug syndicate in Marseilles because of his daughter's drug-related death. Pryor supported black star Max Julien in *The Mack,* a violent melodrama about a California pimp who takes on both white and black mobsters in his struggle to stay on top. He played a secondary pimp. Pryor then supported Zalman King in *Some Kind of Loving.* And in *Uptown Saturday Night,* a bodacious comedy that spawned a whole legion of imitators, he played a private detective, "Sharp Eye Washington," on the trail of the screen's entire pantheon of black superstars – Sidney Poitier, Harry Belafonte and Bill Cosby.

And the *New York Times'* esteemed critic, Vincent Canby, was telling his readers: "Richard Pryor has succeeded in being the best thing in every film I've so far seen him in, with the exception of *Lady Sings the Blues,* which starred Diana Ross. (He was second best in that one.)"

Since 1976, though he has occasionally done a cameo role when the film was a group effort with which he wished to be associated, Richard Pryor has been irrefutably, indisputably, unrestrainedly a superstar.

He is, furthermore, the personification of a particular state of the black experience in America: a direct, albeit aggressively hostile descendant of the black vaudeville with its ethnic stereotypes and dialect humor.

He has made a lasting impression on the face of American popular culture. He has the rare ability to both entertain and, at the same time, say something cogent about the life and times we occupy.

And he is fortunate to have been born when he was.

What makes his comedy work is a hard edge of reality, a

sense of frustration and a potential for violence. At no other time, in no other era in the entire history of show business and/or motion pictures, would his particularly unique contribution have been acceptable. Nor, one suspects, could he have adapted to conditions prevailing in the entertainment world prior to his own generation.

Until the 1890s, nearly all black entertainers were minstrels, singing songs such as "All Coons Look Alike to Me" (written, incidentally, by a black performer) and "Every Race Has a Flag But the Coon," relying on the grotesque minstrel grins and "Yousah, yousah" patter that were so pleasing and nonthreatening to whites. And they imitated whites who, with ludicrous exaggeration, imitated them.

George Walker, a noted turn-of-the-century black comedian once wrote: "Black-faced white comedians used to make themselves look as ridiculous as they could when portraying a 'darky' character. In their makeup they always had tremendously big red lips, and their costumes were frightfully exaggerated. The one fatal result of this to the colored performers was that they imitated the white performers in their make-up as 'darkies.' Nothing seemed more absurd than to see a colored man making himself ridiculous in order to portray himself."

It is impossible to picture Richard Pryor in this milieu.

Nor can a valid parallel be drawn between Pryor's use of the word "nigger" and the fact that George Walker and his comic partner, Bert Williams, became famous by billing themselves as the "Two Real Coons." Unlike Pryor, their motive for employing the hated epithet was mainly professional opportunism.

As Walker once said of that theatrical era, "Black-faced white comedians were numerous and very popular. They billed themselves 'coons.' Bert and I watched the white 'coons,' and were often much amused at seeing white men with black cork on their faces trying to imitate black folks. Nothing about these white men's actions was natural. . . .

"We thought that as there seemed to be a great demand for black faces on the stage, we would do all we could to get what we felt belonged to us by the laws of nature. . . . As white men with black faces were billing themselves 'coons,' Williams and Walker would do well to bill themselves as 'Two Real Coons,' and so we did . . . (and) . . . made us first hit. . . ."

In 1904, Biograph Company made two short films that became milestones in the history of black movies. The first of these comedies was *A Bucket of Cream Ale*. In it, as film historian Eileen Landay has noted, "a white customer angrily shouts at a black waitress for taking a sip from his pitcher. She watches, listens, then pours the contents over his head. The film is over and with it a brief, almost forgotten victory. In no other movie for the next forty years was the black given a chance to fight back."

The other significant Biograph comedy, *A Nigger in the Woodpile*, introduced the stereotype of the black as lazy, stupid, childish and dishonest.

The film opens with a white man sawing wood and piling it in cords in a farmyard. Enter another white with a box of dynamite. They drill a hole in one of the sticks of wood, insert a stick of dynamite in it, then place this on the stack and leave. Two blacks appear, steal the wood and take it to their cabin. When they put some wood in the stove, it explodes, taking both of them with it. *A Nigger in the Woodpile* ends as the original owner of the wood searches the debris for the two blacks.

Disastrously, this brief, 102-foot film fixed the screen image of blacks for generations to come.

It was followed by scores of other equally offensive silent comedies including the *Rastus* and *Sambo* series, *Coon Town Parade,* and *Coon Town Suffragettes,* which detailed how a group of black washerwomen organized an attempt to keep their shiftless husbands out of saloons.

Richard Pryor would not have been typecast as a molasses-slow, shuffling Sambo with a watermelon grin. Nor would he have fitted into the only other two screen roles available for decades to blacks: the savage (noble or ignoble) and the castrated Uncle.

In three respects – his comic genius, his fame and his brilliant pantomime – the legendary Bert Williams was Richard Pryor's true antecedent in show business. From 1906 to 1922, when he died at age forty-nine, Williams was as celebrated as Pryor is now. He was the toast of Broadway, headlining in the *Ziegfeld Follies,* the first black comic to do so. He was also the first black recording star, the first to appear in a command performance before English royalty, the first to star in motion pictures. He was idolized and lionized. He earned more than the President of the United States. W.C. Fields once called him "the funniest man I ever saw and the saddest man I ever knew."

Richard Pryor would not wish to have traded places with Bert Williams, the comedian from whom black-faced artists Al Jolson and Eddie Cantor learned their craft.

A West Indian of light complexion, Williams was forced to "black up" with burnt cork to be accepted by white audiences. Says Eileen Landay, Williams was "trapped by the times behind his black-face mask. He often declared his ambition to 'stop doing piffle and interpret the *real* Negro on the stage.' But it never happened."

Celebrated though he was, he was Jim Crowed everywhere but on the stage—by blacks, since he was of "mixed blood," as well as by whites—resulting in severe chronic depression. This condition was aggravated by his failure as a motion picture star.

His *Darktown Jubilee* (1914) represented the movie industry's first attempt to star a black in a film. Misjudging the temper of the times, Williams made the error of doffing his black-face mask and appearing as "himself"; light-skinned, handsome, and dapper in top hat and tails. At its opening, white patrols—accustomed only to seeing Williams or any other black in Tom roles—jeered the film off the screen, precipitating a race riot.

Two years later, reverting to black-face, Bert Williams made a series of short comedies for Biograph including *A Natural Born Gambler,* based on a famous stage routine of his. No race riots ensued, nor did motion picture stardom.

Black comedy stereotypes prevailed in Hollywood movies throughout the '20s and '30s. Among them were the funny—actually they were—little black children: Farina, Buckwheat, and Stymie, in Hal Roach's "Our Gang" comedies (later retagged *The Little Rascals* for TV). Also, there were Willie "Sleep 'n Eat" Best, Mantan Moreland, and Jack Benny's "Rochester," Eddie Anderson. But for garnering laughs in the unenlightened 1930s, no one beat out Stepin Fetchit, Hollywood's first full-fledged black star, and surely the most famous victim in history of Hollywood's penchant for stereotyping the black race.

Between 1928 and 1939, when he left Hollywood, though returning for a few later films, Stepin Fetchit (*né* Lincoln Theodore Perry) was the top-featured, high-salaried black comic in thirty-six pictures: *Hearts in Dixie, Showboat, In Old Kentucky, Stand Up and Cheer, Carolina, Charlie Chan in Egypt, The Virginia Judge, Dimples, et al.,* plus the four in which he co-starred with Will Rogers, *David Harum, Judge Priest, County Chairman,* and *Steamboat 'Round the Bend.*

In each of them he was the pluperfect prototype for one of Richard Pryor's most outlandish characters. In none of them was he anyone Richard Pryor would care to play on the screen. And in all of them he was the same. Lanky. Bald. Shabbily dressed. Simple-minded. Whining. Clownish. Sleepy-eyed. Self-demeaning. Slow-witted. With it all, though, he was a great comic, a master of stylization.

White moviegoers relished Stepin Fetchit's antics, self-deluding themselves into believing he truly represented the "typical" American black. Blacks knew better, and turned their backs on him.

Stepin Fetchit played the fool and laughed all the way to Hollywood's Bank of America. For a decade he lived in high style. Once the owner of twelve cars (including a pink Cadillac), and the employer of sixteen Chinese servants, he lost his riches in the early 1940s. And there was to be no true comeback for him as his comedy style rapidly went out of fashion. Now, however, his comic characterization is subject to reevaluation.

"When Fetchit's work is viewed today," notes black film historian Donald Bogle, "the subtleties of his performances are more than apparent. As he stands with head hanging and eyes half-closed, not responding to an insult, Stepin Fetchit removes his characters from the real world of petty injustices and racist inhumanities and shows them withdrawing into their self-protective shells. For years such withdrawal was the only way black Americans managed to survive.... His withdrawal indicates an overriding, often excruciating nihilism. This nihilistic aspect might explain in part his popularity in a disillusioned age. Yet it could not save him."

What's more, Bogle continues, "Contrary to opinion today, Stepin Fetchit did not play a placid Tom.... Rather, Stepin Fetchit's characters were coons, those lazy, forever-in-hot-water, natural-born comedian Negroes. Fetchit became the arch-coon, introducing to the screen a repertoire of antics and flamboyant poses that younger black comedians have used ever since."

Stepin Fetchit, eighty-nine now, ill, and living at the Motion Picture Country Home in California, has been saying as much for years.

In 1968, on a series titled *Black History: Lost, Strayed or Stolen*, hosted by Bill Cosby, CBS presented a segment that characterized Stepin Fetchit, so the veteran comedian claimed, as "the white man's Negro, the traditional lazy, stupid, crap-shooter, chicken-stealing idiot," as well as "the epitome of the black man who sold out his people."

Fetchit filed a three million dollar suit against the network, the show's producers and its sponsor, saying, "Like Charlie Chaplin, I played the part of a simple, sincere, honest and lovable character who won sympathy from an audience by being tolerant of those who hurt him so that he could do good for those he loved. I opened the door to the black men of America. If I let this suit go, the same thing can happen to Sammy Davis Jr., Bill Cosby and Sidney Poitier."

In Indianapolis, Indiana, where the comedian was then living and where the suit was filed, U.S. District Court Judge William Steckler dismissed the complaint. He ruled that Fetchit was a public figure through his movies and subject to broadcast comment. The judge also said his privacy had not been invaded and that the remarks of the broadcast were directed only at his role as Fetchit and not at Lincoln Theodore Perry in private life.

Stepin Fetchit took his complaint all the way to the U.S. Supreme Court, hoping to get a jury trial, which was denied.

Late in 1972, two widely divergent generations—Richard Pryor's and Stepin Fetchit's—conjoined at the Sixth Annual Image Awards of the Beverly Hills-Hollywood Branch of the National Association for the Advancement of Colored People.

At the Hollywood Palladium that evening, *Lady Sings the Blues,* its stars, including Richard Pryor, and its executive producer, made a clean sweep of the year's top honors. In addition to awards for its leading players and producer, *Lady Sings the Blues* was crowned Motion Picture of the Year and won both The President's Award and the first Annual Martin Luther King Jr. Award for outstanding achievement in the world of entertainment, which Coretta King personally presented.

Later in the proceedings, then eighty-year-old Stepin Fetchit was honored with a special Image award for "integrity." At the podium, with great dignity, he took the occasion to defend his role as a black pacemaker in films. He declared, to a warm wave of applause, that when he watches blacks on television and in films now he takes credit for the progress that followed in the wake of his stereotype and his ground-breaking.

In October 1981, Hollywood came through with yet another honor for Stepin Fetchit. This was the American Classic Screen Award presented him by the National Film Society, at a banquet at which director Robert Wise, composer Miklos Rozsa, character actress Margaret Hamilton and star Lana Turner also were honored. On this evening no mention was made that the comedian's screen character has been deplored by the black community. And when the eighty-nine-year-old Stepin Fetchit put aside his crutches to do the shuffle for which he is famous, the ovation he received was deafening.

While Richard Pryor may be among the young comics influenced in some circuitous fashion by Stepin Fetchit, he is a more direct descendant of two protean black comedians who once were standard house-packers at Harlem's legendary Apollo

Theater, Pigmeat Markham, a contemporary of Fetchit's, and Redd Foxx.

Pigmeat Markham, huge in size, has been accurately described as "a virtuoso of the bawdy and the low-down." To succeed as a comic he had to develop an elephant's epidermis to avoid being damaged by black critics who screamed that his comedy was "repulsive" and "smelled to high heaven."

Describing Pigmeat Markham's appeal, one Harlem writer in the '30s might as easily have been writing about Pryor: "His main attraction is his gags, capers, and burlesque of the people who crowd the Apollo from top to bottom to see him render his version of their doings. He gathers his material from the saloons, house-rent parties, street scenes, domestic rifts. . . ."

In *The New Yorker* in the summer of 1981, Jervis Anderson made this perceptive observation: "What the proletarian crowds at the Apollo recognized and applauded in the work of comedians like Pigmeat Markham were facets of their own style and experience. When they howled at what Markham said and did, they were howling at wonderful comic dramatizations of themselves or of certain blacks they happened to know."

Hello there, Richard Pryor.

There is no record that Dewey "Pigmeat" Markham ever worked in Hollywood. But, between 1940–46, he starred in eleven comedy pictures made for theaters patronized exclusively by black audiences: *Am I Guilty?, Fight That Ghost, Hell Cats, House Rent Party, Junction 88, Mr. Smith Goes Ghost, One Big Mistake, Pigmeat Markham's Laugh Hepcats, Shut My Big Mouth* (not the Hollywood feature starring Joe E. Brown), *Swanee Showboat,* and *The Wrong Mr. Right.*

Richard Pryor may have seen some of the later ones when first released, though he would have been quite young, but it seems a safe bet that he has bought and studied copies of Pigmeat Markham's films in more recent years.

Of Redd Foxx, for whom Pryor once wrote a number of *Sanford and Son* scripts, there can be no doubt about Foxx's comedic influence on the younger comic. (Incidentally, Foxx's own early influences, at least at the start, were such radio stars as Fred Allen and George Burns, who were popular in his youth.)

Running away from St. Louis, his home town, at seventeen, John Elroy Sanford hopped a freight to New York. He served a long, hustling-for-a-living apprenticeship in show business, including a three-year emcee stint at Gamby's, a club in Baltimore, while developing his racy act as a stand-up comic. He

traveled the black vaudeville circuit, known as the Chitlin'
Circuit, for years; three of them were as a team with Slappy
White. And he perfected the "blue" material for which, away
from the confines of television, he is still best known – risque,
irreverent, double-entendre comments on race, politics and,
especially and always, sex.

Until he was forty-three, though, Redd Foxx was still not
successful enough to earn a full-time living as a comedian, having
to alternate nightclub engagements with a part-time job as a sign
painter.

In that year, 1955, his financial fortunes took a sharp
upscale leap. Dootsie Williams, owner of Dooto Records, a black
firm, caught Redd Foxx's act at the Brass Rail, a downtown Los
Angeles club, and offered him the chance to record *Laff of the
Party*. This was followed by thirty-four more wickedly humorous
party records on the Dooto label, which sold phenomenally well,
winning him a huge national following, particularly among
blacks, and a considerable reputation as a sharp wit whose
insight and faultless timing made him a master of the devilishly
risque story.

Back in Peoria, long before he ever saw Redd Foxx in
person, these party records, followed by another fourteen
recorded for Frank Sinatra's Reprise label, made a lasting
impression on would-be comic Richard Pryor. For in those
X-rated albums, Redd Foxx took huge risks that no black
comedian ever dared take before. He didn't give a fuck about
what anybody thought.

When Redd Foxx inevitably segued into the bigger,
"mixed" clubs, white audiences readily accepted the comedian
and his "blue" act in toto. Unlike other black comics, such as
Pryor, he never had to suffer the indignity of having to adjust his
material to suit the crowd. Not, at least, until he went into
television. At the outset, though, he ventured forth with
trepidation.

In 1959 he played for his first predominantly white
audience at New York's popular Basin Street East. "I was scared
at first," Foxx says, "because I didn't know how far I could go.
Then someone told me, 'Just do your regular thing.' I did, and
tore up the joint. Within a year I'd played my first date in Vegas."

From there, it was steadily onward and upward – playing
only the best clubs at ever bigger salaries until, in 1970, bookers
for the Hilton International Hotel chain in Las Vegas signed him
to a three-year contract paying $960,000 for a minimum of
thirty-two performing weeks a year. And TV's *Sanford and Son*,

a success from its premiere episode, came along less than two years later.

During its five-year run, this television series may well have achieved the goal Redd Foxx had in mind. As he told Leonard Feather when his show rode high in the Nielsens, "I have a lot of faith in the power of humor. I'm convinced that *Sanford and Son* shows middle class America a lot of what they need to know. We're really a common people speaking two different languages, and we have to communicate. The show is lighthearted, it doesn't drive home a lesson, but it can open up people's minds enough for them to see how stupid every kind of prejudice can be. Sanford has his hang-ups, his own kind of prejudices, and while they're laughing at him, the people watching him will get a message."

Still, Redd Foxx could not bear being permanently Sanfordized. He had to break out, and not only come up for air but turn the air blue in the manner to which he had long been accustomed. Sometimes, at no pay, he would play little clubs in and around Hollywood, because "I have to remind my in-person customers that Redd Foxx was around the nightclub circuit for twenty-six years before I turned into that old junkman. Besides, I just have to have that change of pace." Later he embarked on a concert tour with his *Redd Foxx Show*, which was so very "blue" that contracts for the enterprise specified that the show had to be advertised "For Adults Only."

This was, and is, the Redd Foxx closest to Richard Pryor's heart.

Before he had ever heard of Redd Foxx, though, back in the '40s when he was six or eight, Richard Pryor was haunting the movie houses of Peoria and picking up the comedy rhythms of some surprising models.

There were no black comedians of consequence on Hollywood's screens then, with the possible exception of Eddie "Rochester" Anderson. So the youngster was seeing and being influenced by Smiley Burnette, Fuzzy Knight and Pat Buttram (Western sidekicks all), Abbott and Costello, Red Skelton, Jerry Lewis and, more importantly, animated cartoons.

Some Saturdays, for ten cents, he sat mesmerized through a matinee featuring as many as twenty-five cartoons. The result, as one student of his comedy style notes, is that "Pryor's face is trained not to miss a single beat in its union with the rhythms of his characters' speech. In his mind, he has integrated frame after frame of emotional nuance demonstrated by cartoon figures as they encounter seemingly insurmountable obstacles."

Pryor's present-day power to convince audiences of the reality of his characters may well have been born of his willingness to believe in the utter reality of what he saw on the screen as a child, even though it did sometimes lead to disillusionment.

"One of my first big traumatic experiences," he said, "was when I went to see a Little Beaver movie (starring child actor Bobby Blake who later became TV's Robert "Baretta" Blake). When it was over, I tried to get back behind the screen. I thought Little Beaver would be there, you know. And I wanted to talk to him. I never thought to myself, 'Little Beaver's white.' I didn't think about color – just feelings." Then he ruefully adds, "My heroes at the movies were the same as anyone else's. I wanted to be John Wayne too. I didn't know John Wayne hated my guts."

While Richard Pryor, who used to paste his name over Marlon Brando's on movie billboards, continued to harbor his dream of "getting into the movies," the humorless pictures of the '50s and '60s gave neither him nor any other black much to laugh about.

Like a beacon of hope, though, Sidney Poitier arrived on the scene in 1951's *No Way Out*, becoming the first major-grade "serious" black actor. He would go on to star in dozens of worthy films: *A Raisin in the Sun, A Patch of Blue, In the Heat of the Night, Guess Who's Coming to Dinner, et al.* He would become the first black male to be nominated for – and the only one to date to win – an Academy Award, in 1963's *Lilies of the Field.* And he justifiably made blacks proud.

"Poitier," as Pauline Kael observes, "has always had drama going on under the surface of his roles – you could sense the pressures, the intelligence, and the tension of self-control in his characters; that's part of why he became the idealized representative of black people. . . . [He] was able to bring new, angry dignity to black screen acting because of the angry dignity inside him."

Eventually there would come a tendency to downgrade his role as a torchbearer, but Sidney Poitier undeniably paved the way for all who followed him: Harry Belafonte, the first black male sex symbol (whose love scenes with Joan Fontaine in *Island in the Sun*, considered daring and provocative at the time, are mild compared to those of Richard Pryor and Margot Kidder in *Some Kind of Hero*); Calvin Lockhart; Richard Roundtree; Raymond St. Jacques; Paul Winfield; James Earl Jones; Billy Dee Williams; and, yes, Richard Pryor.

But, between the debut of Sidney Poitier and that of Richard Pryor, Hollywood, the movies, and, indeed, the world would have to undergo convolutions and revolution before the screen would be sufficiently enlightened to welcome the likes of a comedian/actor like Richard Pryor.

In the decades between, there were, first, cinematic attempts to come to grips with the ordeal and struggle of Black America, but these films, created almost exclusively by whites, were made without ever consulting black people, without ever asking them what their lives were like.

The real black world was an invisible realm that lay somewhere between limbo and purgatory. Even the inhabitants of this twilight land did not wish to see it depicted on the screen. They wanted to detach themselves, their ambition and their dreams from the sub-world in which they were forced to live. They had set their faces instead toward the land of "Light and White," which, television told them, was "where it was at."

Then history stepped in and caught everything up in a kaleidoscopic series of events. Social change began in America when a middle-aged black woman in Alabama decided that enough was enough and refused to give up her seat on a bus, giving rise to Martin Luther King Jr., who begat Stokely Carmichael, who begat Rap Brown, who begat Huey Newton, who begat Eldridge Cleaver, Bobby Seale and others. Out of the maelstrom emerged a proud new Black Man. Black, he concluded, was beautiful and hip.

Blacks fashioned a new image of themselves for themselves, examining with a most jaundiced eye everything they had been told, read about or seen in a movie.

As black writer Earl Morgan has noted, "Since nothing was to escape the cleansing torch of raised consciousness, films had to come under the gun. Black people were in a mood to see themselves as heroes. They wanted the ubiquitous eye of the camera to turn itself upon the reality they knew, exposing the rawness and pain, the pithy, bittersweet pathos of what had come to be known as the ghetto."

They asked for and got films which, if not about themselves, were at least about certain modern-day blacks they knew or had read about. For a while almost any new film with a scenario involving the black experience was pretty much a guaranteed financial, if not aesthetic, success. For a while black audiences cheered the smooth, in-control, laid-back and street-smart brothers they encountered in movies like *Shaft, Superfly,* and Melvin Van Peebles' *Sweet Sweetback's Baaadasss Song,* films featuring sex and violence. Finally, reaction set in. Many came to agree with the black writer, angered by Van Peebles' film, who declared, "If black people are still in a bag where they get their jollies watching cops get killed in the movies, we're in bad shape."

Interestingly, though Pryor had little affection for such films, being partial to upbeat films himself – films offering positive images of blacks – he did not join those black leaders who condemned "blaxploitation" pictures. They vigorously reacted to these frequently tawdry cinematic portraits of blacks as pimps (which Pryor sometimes played), prostitutes, drug dealers and studs. But he argued, "Movies are movies, and I don't think any of them are going to hurt the moral fiber of America and all that nonsense. The black groups that boycott certain films would do better to get the money together to make the films they want to see, or stay in church and leave us to our work."

Black exploitation films began failing at the box-office. It was time for a different kind of film. It was time for laughter, as well as reality, in an uncensored era of total freedom on the screen. It was time for Richard Pryor. Almost.

In 1973, after paying his dues in toned-down movie roles for years, Pryor was certain the time had come for him to burst forth, without restraints, as a star in the riotous Western spoof *Blazing Saddles*, which he helped Mel Brooks write. (They later shared two honors for the screenplay of *Blazing Saddles*; the American Writers' Guild Award and the American Academy of Humor Award.) But the tailor-made role of the sheriff was denied him, to the regret of critics such as Pauline Kael, who wrote: "Pryor's demons are what make people laugh. If he had played the sheriff in *Blazing Saddles*, he'd have made him *crazy* – threatening and funny, both." Then, as an after-thought, she added, "Pryor shouldn't be cast at all – he should be realized. He has desperate, mad characters coming out his pores, and we want to see how far he can go with them."

Pryor's anger at losing the role in *Blazing Saddles*, "a historic blast of derision at the heroic myths of the Old West," is still directed mainly at Mel Brooks.

When a *Gallery* reporter asked if he liked Mel Brooks as a person, Pryor's reply was: "No. He hurt me. He lied to me. He didn't have the decency to call me up and tell me I wasn't going to star in *Blazing Saddles*. And what hurt me about it was that I was in the car with Cleavon Little and Billy Dee Williams and we were going to a nightclub. They asked what I was doing. Naturally, I said I was going to do *Blazing Saddles*. And the funny thing is, Cleavon had already been signed for the part. You know what I mean? Shit. Brooks was supposed to call me up and at least tell me that I didn't get the part."

To yet another reporter, Pryor maintained that he had

played the major role in writing the film, on which three other screenwriters also worked, but didn't get proper credit. "They used me and that's not fair," he said. "And it's a thorn in my heart about it."

Speaking of Pryor, the other writers, Andrew Bergman, Norman Steinberg and Alan Unger, and Mel Brooks himself said to Kenneth Tynan, shortly before that esteemed critic's death: "For nine months, we worked together like maniacs. We went all the way – especially Richard Pryor, who was very brave and very far-out and very catalytic." Brooks added that they "wrote berserk, heartfelt stuff about white corruption and racism and Bible-thumping bigotry. We used dirty language on the screen for the first time, and to me the whole thing was like a big psychoanalytic session."

In his *New Yorker* profile of Brooks, which subsequently appeared in his book *Show People*, Kenneth Tynan details what happened next: "Warners snapped up the completed script and hired Brooks to direct his first Hollywood movie. There was one stipulation: the campfire sequence, in which the bean-fed cowpokes audibly befoul the night air, must be cut. Brooks and his colleagues stood firm: either the scene stayed or they quit. Here, and elsewhere in the screenplay, they saw no reason to disown what is called 'healthy vulgarity' when it occurs in Chaucer, and 'childish smut' when it infiltrates the cinema. Eventually the studio gave in. . . . Casting, however, was not without problems. Brooks wanted Richard Pryor to play the black protagonist. . . . Warners rejected Pryor, whom they thought too undisciplined. Cleavon Little (a suave performer with no flair for comedy) got the job instead."

Blazing Saddles might have made Richard Pryor a star overnight. But it did nothing of the sort for Cleavon Little.

Late in 1981, when Little returned to New York to live and to rehearse an Off-Broadway play, *The Resurrection of Lady Lester,* the disillusioned actor told a reporter, "My film career never was what it should have been based on the success of that movie. I'm not sure why. I was disappointed. Finally, *Blazing Saddles* got to be like an albatross too, because people figured, well, he can't do anything but comedy. I wound up making some movies just so I could eat. I felt that if you have the chance to do something, it's better to do something than *nothing*, especially if you're doing nothing *a lot*."

And, if it's any consolation to Richard Pryor, Mel Brooks still salutes him for possessing "almost Nietzschean ideals of what is good, what is powerful, what is superior."

In the few years since he became a uniquely potent box-office name, following 1976's *Adios Amigo* (which he actively loathes), Pryor has starred in thirteen films. For what they reveal about him as a developing, constantly maturing artist, the one major black actor/comedian working steadily in film today, they are worth considering individually.

The Bingo Long Traveling All-Stars and Motor Kings
(1976; Universal)

Pryor was a "hired" actor, billed third, in this release, a flip and funky Depression days comedy about life in the old Negro National (baseball) League. He was seen as Charlie Snow, the team's hustling third baseman, who hilariously tried to pass himself off as a Cuban (or, as he put it, "Koo-bin"), then as an Indian, in a desperate effort to crash the all-white major leagues. *Playboy*, pegging it as an "offbeat, soul-warming social comedy," singled out Pryor and James Earl Jones for honors. But Pryor, lacking control over the project, saw much of his comedy efforts end up on the cutting room floor to allow more footage for sex symbol Billy Dee Williams, the top-ranked star.

Car Wash *(1976; Universal)*

In this frantic, hyperactive, free-wheeling comedy, featuring a huge, alphabetically billed, mostly black cast, and set exactly where you'd expect it to be set, Pryor was the flashy divine in the gold Rolls-Royce, who preached the eternal verity of the all-mighty dollar. His acting, said *Time*, was the only thing to remember about this film. Nearly all the critics sided with the one who sniffed that it was "the movie equivalent of junk food." *Car Wash* made money, but Richard Pryor still had not hit his stride.

Silver Streak *(1976; 20th Century-Fox)*

Playing a lovable conman in this mystery comedy set aboard a train from Los Angeles to Chicago, Pryor shared co-star billing with Gene Wilder (they would be teamed again) and proved he was box-office dynamite even though he did not appear on screen until the movie was half over. But the second half is all that anyone cares to remember about *Silver Streak*, even though the funniest scene is a throwback to "objectionable" black humor of the '30s. In escaping the bad guys, Gene Wilder dons black-face makeup while new buddy Pryor instructs this hopelessly unenlightened white in the ways of black cool. Pryor looked back on this movie, and particularly this black-face episode, with regret. "I put myself in *Silver Streak* but I didn't do it, not with my heart," he said. "It was a business decision. I was looking to hustle, and I got hustled. They felt that having a real black actor in the movie would sort of make it all right. So I'm the token black, a modern Willie Best. It was a career move, and I'm not sorry I did it. But. . . ." Critic Pauline Kael, chastising the moviemakers, got to the heart of the problem in her review, saying of Pryor: "He saves their picture for a few minutes – he gives it some potency and turns it into the comedy they hoped for – and they emasculate him, turn him into a lovable black man whose craziness is only a put-on. Interracial brotherly love is probably the one thing that Richard Pryor should never be required to express. It violates his demonic, frazzled blackness."

Greased Lightning *(1977; Warner Bros.)*

In the true-life story of the first black champion race-driver, Wendell Scott, a light drama with only incidental humor, Pryor received star billing for the first time, above Cleavon *(Blazing Saddles)* Little, Pam Grier and Beau Bridges. There was something of Pryor himself in this story of a man who broke the color barrier and realized his dream despite bigotry. "He's a special kind of people," Pryor has said of Scott. "When he was a kid, they told him the rules. They said, 'You can't cross that street over there until the light changes.' And he said, 'I understand all that, but *excuse* me.' And he went and crossed the street. And he didn't get hit by no car – nothin' happened. So he made the rest of the kids feel stupid for listenin'." Said *The Christian Science Monitor* film critic David Sterritt, who had reservations about the picture, "Pryor is most charming in his comparatively straightforward role, and as credible as his material allows." Richard Pryor has said it was the first worthwhile starring role anyone had offered him. He also says magnanimously of co-star Beau Bridges: "He was wonderful. I'd watch him in a close-up and want to kill him, he was so good. He taught me a lot about acting in front of the camera."

Which Way Is Up? *(1977; Universal)*

This was a Hollywood variation on Italy's *The Seduction of Mimi*, Lina Wertmuller's comedy about sex and politics, with the scene shifted to the strife-torn farm country of Central California. Pryor essayed a tour de force triple role here: a beleaguered Fresno grape picker who finds himself on the slippery ladder of success; his cotton-headed, dirty-minded old father; and a two-timing, hypocritical preacher – of the "7-11 Lucky Church of External Salvation"—who declares that "teeth decay from sin and lust and I have no cavities." The comic found the critics lying in wait for him. "Excess—too much of the good thing Pryor is—is the problem," ranted Judith Crist, whose opinion was echoed by others. She also asserted that the scriptwriters failed him by substituting "too many stock situations for social satire, and too much and too heavy-handed sex comedy for the light-hearted consideration of politics, women's lib and machismo that gave substance to the delightful original." *Which Way Is Up?* was Pryor's first film under his unique contract with Universal, guaranteeing him three million dollars over four years, calling for his services as performer and/or writer, giving him a share of the profits of each film in which he acted, and permitting him to make pictures for other companies. Said a Universal studio executive upon the signing of the contract, "We believe it is possible to make money on class A pictures that not only star black people, but are made by black people." And Pryor cracked: "Well, I guess that means if these movies don't make money a whole lot of niggers gonna be in trouble." *Which Way Is Up?* was a box-office winner.

Blue Collar *(1978; Universal)*

A contemporary drama about Detroit auto workers, done totally without humor in the *film noir* style of nightmare realism, *Blue Collar* was fraught with problems during production (Pryor fought with director Paul Schrader and his co-stars), but, despite its depressing theme, won favor with reviewers and audiences. Its downbeat story line was that of three ordinary men—two blacks (Pryor and Yaphet Kotto) and one white (Harvey Keitel)—whose impulsive decision to rob their own union results in tragic consequences for each of them. Pryor was the beaten-down, corruptible turncoat who eventually sold out his partners to the union officials. He hated the character he played. "I lived with that every day for ten weeks, knowing what he was going to do," he said, "and it was really hard." Just before the film's release, Pryor said, "It changed my life. I had a whole struggle going on—getting that deep, revealing that pain. It's scary. People are going to come in expecting laughs and they'll see this different side of me. I don't want to be used to bring in the black audience and then to have them devastated. They have to be prepared. I don't think I could stand the rejection." Apparently they were properly prepared for this drama, stating that the system grinds all workers down, for shouts of "Right on!" were heard in darkened movie houses across the land.

The Wiz *(1978; Universal)*

Pryor gained little or no ground in this modernized, hip musical version of *The Wizard of Oz*, with its all-star black cast: Diana Ross, Nipsey Russell (who, as the Tin Woodman, stole all the reviews), Michael Jackson, Lena Horne, Ted Ross and Mabel King. The title role, which Pryor played, almost certainly as a favor to Motown mogul Berry Gordy Jr., who gave him his break in an earlier Motown production, *Lady Sings the Blues*, has always been the story's least impressive part. Noting that "as the con-man Wiz, Richard Pryor begins entertainingly, but his role peters out," *The New Yorker* critic added, "Pryor, with his spooked look, which gives a tension to whatever he does, seems such an obvious choice for the Cowardly Lion [played by Ted Ross] that the casting appears a little off." To be a winner, however, *The Wiz* would have needed more than recasting.

California Suite *(1978; Columbia)*

Pauline Kael termed the entire film, consisting of four separate Neil Simon comedy skits with a Beverly Hills Hotel locale, an "acute embarrassment." But she took particular umbrage at the segment featuring black stars. In this slapstick playlet, she wrote, "Richard Pryor and Bill Cosby [working together for the first time since *Uptown Saturday Night*] are vacationing doctors from Chicago who, with their wives (Gloria Gifford and Sheila Frazier), get into a mixed-doubles brawl. On the stage, this material—in which the actors squabble, turn belligerent, and have a knock-down-drag-out fight, from which they all emerge battered and bandaged—was played by white actors. But, since these are the only misfits in the hotel, when the roles are played by black actors the skit seems to be saying that the men may be doctors but they're still uncontrollable, dumb blacks who don't belong in a rich, civilized atmosphere; and the recessive whitened decor turns them into tar babies. When they don't know how to handle cars, when they stumble around a flooded room, crash into each other, step on broken glass, or, even worse, when Cosby bites Pryor's nose, it all has horrifying racist overtones." Despite all, audiences went to see it, and laughed, and turned *California Suite* into a monster success.

Richard Pryor Live in Concert *(1979; Special Event Entertainment)*

You need look no further to find Richard Pryor's favorite film to date. Filmed at a concert he gave in Long Beach, California, late in 1978, containing material new and old (from the album *Wanted: Richard Pryor*), this is eighty minutes of pure (or impure) Pryor. The funniest, filthiest-talking, most unpredictable entertainer in the world lets it all hang out here. Roaming the stage like a wildman sage, he takes off on his marital problems, his entanglements with the law, the difference between black and white funerals, sexual monkeys, the ring performance of boxer Leon Spinks, Muhammad Ali, male-female sexual relationships, hunting, his father's strict sense of discipline, etc. Moreover, *Live in Concert* has one thing you don't get from albums and only sparingly in other movies – the visual image of Pryor, the great comic of our age, in all his madness, making outrageous faces, jogging, flopping to the stage floor and gesturing obscenely at the audience. So outrageous is *Live in Concert* that its producer felt compelled to insert this in all its newspaper ads: "WARNING: This picture contains harsh and very vulgar language and may be considered shocking and offensive." Said Pryor at the time, "I think that's a good idea, to have that warning. I have a vision of little old ladies coming into the theater by mistake and having coronaries." Asked why he made the film, the comedian answered, "Money, pure greed. Also, to have my art etched in celluloid and shown 'round the world. Most of all, greed." Believe the middle part, Loving money as he does, he loves his art more. "I love what I do very much," he said. "It's the only thing in my life that's never hurt me, that's given me my fulfillment, and let me have my dignity. Never belittled me. I'll be all right as long as they have show business. If they change that around – if they stop laughing – I don't want to live."

The Muppet Movie *(1979; AFD)*
Pryor did a cameo role as a balloon-seller at a fair.

Wholly Moses *(1980; Columbia)*
"Wholly cow," said *Variety*, not complimentarily. This failed comedy starred Dudley Moore as "a false ancient religious saviour named Herschel, who overhears God's instructions to Moses and assumes the assignment to lead his people out of slavery." Pryor was only in for a guest turn as Pharaoh. Luckily.

Stir Crazy *(1980; Columbia)*
The biggie. The blockbuster toward which Richard Pryor had been heading like a homing pigeon for a decade. In this off-the-wall, over-the-wall comedy, Sidney *(Uptown Saturday Night)* Poitier was again his director, and Gene Wilder once more his co-

star. The highly compatible comics played a pair of New York show business hopefuls, driving across the country to the more promising shores of California, who become stranded in a small backwater town. To make some quick dough, they take a job as singing-dancing woodpeckers to promote the opening of a new bank. Which is when their troubles begin. Their feathered costumes are stolen by a pair of hoods who stage a daring daylight hold-up at the bank. Logically presumed to be the culprits, and having no alibi, Wilder and Pryor are given the traditional sentence for bank robbery in that township: 125 years. When you're suddenly thrown in the can, surrounded by the dregs of society, how do you cope? In Pryor's brain, the answer is obvious: when in stir, do as the stirrees. As they enter a holding cell which resembles nothing so much as the locker room below the Roman coliseum during Caligula's reign, he points out to a paranoid, petrified Wilder: "You gotta be baaaad. Walk baaaad, talk baaaad, look baaaad, and nobody's gonna hassle you." Wilder tries. He struts. He snarls. He narrows his eyes like Bogart gazing at the last plane to Marseilles. But somehow, he just doesn't have the rhythm. The rest of the comedy's fun is provided by the visual mishaps of the pair as they get accustomed to life behind bars and plot their eventual escape. Richard Pryor rated and received this deep bow from *Variety*: "*Stir Crazy* succeeds because of Pryor. His pained look into the camera when he's sentenced to jail, his hopeless reactions to Wilder's eccentricities and his overall stance as the famed fool make a flimsy feature like *Stir Crazy* worth seeing. To quote an often used line, 'That takes talent.'" *Stir Crazy*, winning great favor with white audiences as well as the huge black audience Pryor's long had in his hip pocket, earned a mint.

Bustin' Loose *(1981; Universal)*

For the first time Pryor wrote (the original story), produced and starred in a film. A gentle romantic comedy, *Bustin' Loose* is the tale of an ex-con (Pryor) and a schoolteacher (Cicely Tyson), who transport eight children from a Philadelphia ghetto to the tranquillity of a small farm outside Seattle, Washington. Begun before the fire that nearly claimed his life, *Bustin' Loose* was completed after his release from the hospital, and may have been flawed by the break in production. Most critics cited it as a second-rate *African Queen*, since Pryor plays a slob (like Bogart) forced to use his ingenuity to save a prim, prudish female (like Hepburn), as all the while they are falling in love, one becoming nicer, the other looser. "It's a family movie with a formula plot and a horribly corny ending, and the movie almost succeeds in domesticating Richard Pryor – certainly enough to make some of his fans squirm and mutter under their breath," said *New York* magazine critic David Denby. "Yet the whole picture is friendly and good-hearted in ways that are hard to resist."

Some Kind of Hero *(1982; Paramount)*
This comedy-drama is *not* a family movie. Pryor portrays an American soldier who returns home after six years as a POW in Vietnam to find his marriage, his family, in fact his world, have fallen apart. Enter Margot Kidder as an attractive high-class hooker, loaded with wit and style, who happens to like what she does for a living and is well paid for it. Falling in love with Pryor, she helps him adjust to the real world. Enter, too, the steamiest, most graphic love scenes – a bathtub sequence, a strip and a nude-in-bed episode – ever filmed in any interracial love story. Said leading lady Kidder: "They're not pornographic but very, very hot," particularly one scene in which he first brings her character to orgasm. And who would have believed that Richard Pryor could become more controversial than he already was?

RICHARD PRYOR: MOVIE STAR.
Once he said on one of his record albums: "I always wondered if movie stars went to the bathroom. I figured they'd get somebody else to do it for them."
Now, if anyone knows, he does.

6.

DO NOT ASK HOW MANY TIMES RICHARD PRYOR has been married. Different sources, different answers. Three. Five. More? He has four children – none of them the offspring of his most recent marriages to Deboragh McGuire and Jennifer Lee – whose mothers' names are unknown to his public. He likes it that way.

Besides a son, Richard Jr. (b. 1961), who grew up in Peoria, presumably with his mother, the comedian has three daughters: Renee (b. 1957), Elizabeth Ann (b. 1967), and Rain (b. 1969), after whom the production company of Richard Pryor Enterprises, Black Rain, is named.

Who are the mothers of these children? He was asked.

"We care, but we don't want to mention them," said Pryor.

There are two of them?

"More than that."

End of conversation.

Other sources inform that one of his children is "Shelley's (no last name) kid." He had none by Deboragh, and Elizabeth is from his marriage to Maxine (again, no surname).

According to hospital sources, during his recuperation, it was ex-wife Maxine who cut his toenails, which were growing long. "He asked her to cut his toenails and she cut his toenails for him." What are ex-wives for?

It is an inescapable fact that women, a great variety of women, black and white, old and young, have played major roles – possibly even the dominant role – in Richard Pryor's life. The cast of characters is Tolstoyian: grandmother, mother, aunts, prostitutes, nuns, teachers, mentors, friends, wives, fiancees, lovers, and those that might most aptly be termed sex mates.

"I learn from women in my life," he has said.

Indeed.

His education began, surely, as a child growing up in the Peoria whorehouses he has always said his grandmother owned and operated.

As he told Sander Vanocur, "When I was a child, that was what a lot of families did. It was an adventure. It was two worlds.

Women

The world of peeking through the keyhole and looking over transoms, watching things when I didn't exactly know what they were. You had to be an adult – you had to be very careful about what you said because the police might take you away at any moment."

"I knew it was a whorehouse, but I never knew much about the whores," he told Ace Burgess. "I never asked about it; it was all fantasy-like to me." But his sexual curiosity must have been aroused early, for he added, "I used to fuck a lot, but I didn't know what I was doing. When I was five I used to fuck this girl named Mary . . . and when I was nine, this whore gave me some pussy. I think my father had her give me some to see what kind of dude I was."

Later came the girl – no name – he made pregnant in his teens, followed by the wife – apparently his first, again no name – he married at nineteen. Then there were the exotic dancers who were the main attraction at the clubs he played as an aspiring comedian.

On his album *That Nigger's Crazy*, he tells of his uncle, who "only fucked in one position, up and down," and warned him: "Boy, don't you *ever* kiss no pussy. Whatever you do in life, don't you *ever* kiss no pussy." Then comes the big laugh as he adds in his own voice, "I couldn't WAIT to kiss a pussy. He'd been wrong about everything else."

Like so much of his comedy, it seems to have derived from personal experience. He was talking to David Felton of *Rolling Stone* about his Army stint when he confided, "I gave some head for the first time in my life when I was in Germany. That was an experience. I'll never forget how it felt. . . . I knew I would be doing it again."

Apparently this particular Army experience later served him well. When he began playing clubs, he told Felton, it was this way: "Like you'd suck a firedancer's pussy in the dressing room, and her next job she'd try to get you as the MC." Then he added with a laugh: "Shit, if I hadn't been able to give head, probably still be in St. Louis, at the Faust Club."

A sexual creature he has always been, and remains. As he said a while back, "If I ain't horny, I check to see if my heart's beatin'. I am considered a *'pussy man.'* Give me the pussy and I'll deal with the rest of the shit later."

In a more genteel manner he has said, "You take time with women and women will teach you. I think they really are a lot of fun. I like to be in love."

The numerous women Richard Pryor has loved – and/or lived with and/or married – run the color-spectrum gamut: black, white and Asian tawny. In the past, when he has been romantically involved with white women, could it possibly be construed as a subliminal case of "Richard's revenge?" Asked this, Budd Friedman, owner of The Improv where Pryor worked years ago, laughed and said, "Oh, I don't know. But, having met some of these women, I think maybe they were doing a number on him. He didn't get away scot-free."

Confronted by the same query, Rob Cohen, producer of Pryor's *The Wiz*, answered: "Let's put it this way: the hottest sexual relationships with women I've ever had have been with women I'm angry at."

Obviously believing Pryor when he said, "I like to be in love," two newspaper gossip columnists once had him engaged to two different girls, one black, one white, within the same month.

On November 6, 1976, Earl Wilson announced without elaboration, "Richard Pryor and Pam Grier got engaged." Exactly twelve days later, syndicated society columnist Robin Sloan Adams' readers were being informed: "He's given Lucy Saroyan, the daughter of author William Saroyan and stepdaughter of actor Walter Matthau, a great big diamond engagement ring."

Nothing came of Pryor's relationship with Lucy Saroyan, who played the wife of his co-star, Harvey Keitel, in *Blue Collar*. Pam Grier was a different matter.

"I love strong, smart women," Pryor has said, "but I feel inadequate to them." Proof of the truth of both parts of his statement is what happened with his long-term love affair with actress Pam Grier, his wife in *Greased Lightning*, who is undeniably strong and smart.

A statuesque (6') beauty with a voluptuous body (39-24-37), Grier has played a busty, sexily-clad woman of action, acquiring a satin-lady image, in twenty five films like *Black Mama, White Mama* and *Coffy*. Once asked what kind of man she goes for, she seemed to mean Pryor when she answered: "Some of the men I date are shorter than I and not extremely attractive. It's not just a gorgeous body. I think the guy who flaunts it is the guy who has some insecurities about himself. A guy who has fantastic sex appeal is the guy who hides it and cherishes it like a jewel. Right?"

Being the cousin of ex-football star–actor Rosey Grier, it naturally followed that she would be an ace at sports–tennis in her case. Therein lay the seeds of disaster in her romance with Richard Pryor.

When their fling had been flung, *Newsweek*'s Maureen Orth observed: "Pryor has shown a drive not to be bested by anyone. After Pam Grier . . . beat him for a second time at tennis, he wouldn't speak to her for a day. She gave him some suggestions. 'I'm supposed to take instructions and have you beat my ass too?' said Pryor. 'No way.' Instead, he challenged her to game after game. Once, when she fainted in the middle of a match, he got so mad that he stormed off the court."

Up in smoke.

Three months later, in the autumnal equinox of 1977, he married black model Deboragh McGuire, who was eleven years his junior. They'd known one another for three years. She was reportedly his fourth wife, according to *US* magazine, or his fifth, insisted *People*. Pryor once termed it his third marriage–"on paper." Yet, contradicting himself, he told Barbara Walters on TV in 1980: "I have one marriage. I married one person, I married Deboragh. That's my wife. And the rest of them, I said I had 'em 'cause I have children, you know." Did he mean he'd had only one legal marriage? Were the others just women he'd lived with but said he'd married? To both queries, he answered: "Um hmmmm."

Whatever the number, this time it was different, he insisted. "Love came into play. But even more important, Debbie is my life force. This is the first time I've been married–in my heart."

Sounded good.

Deboragh moved in with him at his pink stucco Spanish-style mansion, the old Wrigley Chewing Gum estate, in Northridge in the San Fernando Valley. It was the first house he'd ever owned, with three-and-a-half acres, shaded by fifty-two citrus and nut trees, an Olympic-sized pool (he doesn't swim, and in one of his best-known scenes, he describes how he almost drowned in the pool, to the amusement of his children), screening room, aviary and atrium, two guest cottages, ten-foot-high fence and iron gate, gymnasium, stables, boxing ring, and tennis court, but, since Pryor wouldn't have it, no air-conditioning.

At home, the newlyweds posed domestically for an *Ebony* photographer and Deboragh said, "There are many facets and stages to Richard, and I think I know each of his little roles. I have to sort of get into each personality of his, which is like thirty-five or thirty different people. It's interesting, though. It keeps you on your feet."

Uh-huh.

Four months after the wedding, on New Year's Day 1978, after ramming his Mercedes into her gleaming new Buick Regal, which Deboragh and two women friends of hers quickly vacated, Pryor pumped ten bullets into the empty automobile with his .357 magnum pistol and, as a friend put it, "basically killed the car."

"I thought the situation was hysterically funny at first," Deboragh said later. "Just like a silly movie with everyone bad-mouthing everyone else. But things really got out of hand and Richard blew up."

Divorce number (?).

Between marriages, Pryor once admitted, "For a long time I saw women as sexual objects, and I was always trying to keep from getting hurt. Then one day they would pack up and leave, taking something more with them than their clothes. They took my happiness. Now I'd rather rob a bank than mess with women the way I used to."

In August 1981, Richard Pryor was quietly married to actress Jennifer Lee, who is white.

Richard Pryor literally owes his life to another woman, someone who has known and loved him from the time he was born: his beloved Aunt Dee. He often speaks of her, nearly always citing her saint-like qualities and "pure heart."

On that tragic night of June 9, 1980, when he was suddenly engulfed in flames, his aunt was living with him at his San Fernando Valley house. Fortunately.

As the fire enveloped his body, Pryor said, "I jumped on the bed and grabbed the blanket and tried to put out the fire. Finally, my Aunt Dee came in. She'd heard all the commotion, and she grabbed a sheet and wrapped me up and put out the fire."

Her quick action doubtless saved his life. And he isn't forgetting it.

Yet one woman, more than any of his wives or loves, was the focal point of Richard Pryor's existence until her death in 1978, at seventy-nine. He made this clear when he said, "The biggest moment of my life was when my grandmother was with me on *The Mike Douglas Show*."

Marie Bryant, who operated a brothel and/or merely a poolhall, as some maintain now, was many things to her famous grandson. Guardian. Advice giver. Staunch support. Confidante. Moral arbiter. Consoling shoulder to cry on. Inspiration. The one to whom he looked for approval. The one who tried to save his eternal soul from the clutches of the devil.

"My grandmother, back in Peoria," he once told Henry Allen, "she had arthritis and she used to go to all these tent revivals. She took me with her once, to get the preacher to take the devil out of me. It was kind of embarrassing, in front of all those people, you know.

"He prayed over me, and says for the devil to come out! And I'm thinking, I didn't feel anything, I couldn't see it. Maybe . . . it's still in there. And if you have one, you should keep it with you. It makes you experiment, makes you a sailor, a land sailor, a sailor of hearts."

"My grandmother." She is never far from his thoughts. Count Dracula never ventured forth without his essential box of his native Transylvanian earth. With Richard Pryor, it is the memory of his father's mother. Many conversational paths lead back to her. Like when he talked about his present wealth.

"I'd be a liar if I said I didn't like money," he said. "But if I woke up tomorrow and it was gone or if they took it away from me—and don't you think they *can't*—I'd be fine. The dollar bills can all go. They're not mine anyway, I don't own the printing press. I'd still have the knowledge. My grandmother always told me, 'Son, one thing a white man can't take from you is the knowledge.' " The knowledge, the mysterious inner something, the secret that is a man's own.

Because his grandmother was an affluent business woman, he was born in a hospital, St. Francis Hospital. ("I was meant to be a Catholic, you know.") As he has pointed out, "That was pretty hip to be born in St. Francis, 'cause not many niggers was born in a hospital, in Peoria. Most cats was born at home, in the kitchen."

Pryor, who has said that at least half the dialogue he uses in his material was once actually spoken to him, often does a riff on his grandmother in his act. "My grandmother told me," he says, " 'Don't you put me on no more of those records. You know I don't talk like that!' I say, 'Grandma, you forgot.' "

Grandma brought him up—and strictly. She made him go to church. She made him obey. And, when he warranted it, she meted out the punishment.

He recalls once going out on the Illinois River on a raft with a bunch of pals. The swift current dragged them far from the riverbank and their frantic paddling was to no avail. Since none of them could swim they had to be rescued by a river patrol boat.

"I wished I'd stayed out there on that river when I got back on land," he related. "My grandmother was waiting for me – watchin' in this big bay window that the girls used to tap on. She came out of the house and beat my butt all the way up Washington Street and back into the house. On top of everything, we had built the raft out of my grandmother's fence poles. She whipped my behind *that* day! I ain't been near no raft since."

Pryor returned to Peoria in 1977 to celebrate his thirty-seventh birthday with his grandmother. While there, he complained of chest pains and was admitted to the coronary care unit of the Methodist Medical Center. His grandmother was quoted by reporters as saying, after he was hospitalized, "He's doing as well as can be expected, considering he's had a heart attack."

More recently Pryor has said, "I found out there's nothing wrong with my heart. . . . Wasn't really a heart attack, it was a murmur. But it's no longer there. It reversed itself. Just like when I was in the hospital [after being burned] and one night my kidneys just went out and they thought I was going to die. They were O.K. the next day. Same thing with my heart; the murmur just went away."

His grandmother died in 1978 with his name on her lips.

"I watched her die," he has said. "She died worrying about us, her kids, her people. She looked at me and said, 'Son, you just don't know. It's ugly out there. You've got to protect yourself from it now. You're on your own now, Richard. Be careful.' "

He weeps often when he mentions her name now. He did the day he told an interviewer, *Ebony*'s Managing Editor, Charles L. Sanders, about her dying and its unexpected meaning to him.

"My grandmother's death was very devastating to me," he said. Here he broke down and cried. Recovering his composure, he continued, "I hope people won't misunderstand this, but there's a moment when you're . . . well . . . when you're glad she's dead. You feel that some kind of pressure has been lifted off you, then you feel guilty for feeling that way, then you feel sadness that such a great woman is gone. Does saying that make me an ugly person? I hope not. Do you think people will understand what I'm trying to say about my grandmother?"

Charles L. Sanders then compassionately asked, "Are you trying to say that when she died you were finally able to cut the strings that had tied you to her so closely all your life? You were finally able to be your own man?"

Said Pryor, "That's it, and thanks for understanding. I'd been afraid to say those things about her death. But that's the way I felt . . . that I could finally take care of my own life now."

Of his mother, who "wasn't the strongest person in the world" and who died in 1968, he has said far less than of his Grandma Bryant.

Mostly, he appears to view his mother sympathetically as one of life's unfortunates, who never had a chance to do or be better. "I saw my mother turn tricks for some drunk white man when I was a kid," he said. "I saw my father [who died in 1969] take the money, and I saw what it did to them. They shouldn't have had to do what they did to live."

Then he added in their defense, "But they gave me righteousness, my parents. I'm a good person. Nobody can reproach me on nothing. I didn't cut nobody's throat to get where I am."

Pryor, the father of three daughters and a son, takes pride in being able to take care of them financially and shower them with expensive gifts like the Mercedes-Benz 450SL he presented his eldest, Renee, on one birthday. But "I don't know if I take care of them emotionally," he fretted.

As he explained, "The time I spend with them is very little compared to what I know they need. But I'm their father. I love them . . . but I don't know that I serve any great purpose in their lives other than that of Richard Pryor, the father. Do you understand? I'm not stable. I'm not there. They don't look over the table at me every night. I'd like to be with them every night and hear them say, 'Daddy . . . this' and 'Daddy . . . that.' But they'll be fine because they're fine human beings."

A concerned father, he has also said, "Sometimes I see my faults in my children, and I wish I'd worked harder on myself."

Movie costume designer Sally Hanson, a friend of many years, cites this as an example of Pryor as a loving father: "At the time his daughter Elizabeth was born he swiped her out of the hospital when she was just one day old and brought her over to my house to show me. He was that proud of her. He just had to show me this beautiful little girl of his!"

All four of his children went with him on a 1977 vacation to Europe and Africa, but, of that expedition, he laughs and says, "Never again. There just wasn't enough Daddy to go around."

One of Pryor's choice comedy routines is his *Rumplestiltskin* bit, about some terrified school kids performing the classic fairy tale. It was born, not surprisingly, out of reality, and is something of a tribute to Juliette Whittaker, the woman without whom there might never have been a Richard Pryor, Actor. It is indicative of his affection for her that in 1973, when he won an Emmy for writing the Lily Tomlin television specials, instead of putting it on a mantel, he made a pilgrimage to Peoria to present it to Juliette Whittaker.

Today, Miss Whittaker, a handsome black woman, the daughter of a lawyer and a drama graduate from the University of Iowa, runs a private school for gifted children, The Learning Tree, in Peoria. Richard Pryor has established seventy scholarships for youngsters attending this school. And he has done it for a cause.

When Pryor was a kid – "He was about thirteen but looked ten," she recalls – Miss Whittaker was a supervisor at the Carver Community Center, a public recreation facility which the comic has described as a place "to keep gang fights from happening." Her main responsibility was staging children's plays at the Center.

Already, thanks to movies, he had aspirations to be an actor, but, prior to this teacher's entrance into his life, he'd had no acting experience except what training he got on the streets.

As he once explained to *Rolling Stone*, "It's like, niggers train in a different way. Like, they don't have no theater groups, but niggers train on the corner, you know what I mean? Like when you hang out bullshittin', and singin' and shit?

"We used to have good sessions sometimes. We was doin' it all day to each other, you know? Bang bang – 'Your shoes are run over so much they look like your *ankles* is broke,' and shit like that. I remember once I came up with a beaut, man, I killed them one day. I came up with 'The Rummage Sale Ranger,' you know what I mean? 'cause that's where he got his clothes. 'The Rummage Sale Ranger' – that was a knockout. I saved that one for last, that ended it."

When Juliette Whittaker first spotted Richard hanging around a rehearsal of *Rumplestiltskin*, she invited him to play a servant and gave him the script.

"He came back with the whole script memorized, every part," she has told *Playboy*'s William Brashler. "And when the boy playing the king was absent, Richard took his place. Well, he brought so much new business – new lines and expressions – to the part everybody was amazed. And when the boy playing the king returned and saw him, he let him keep the part. So Richard stayed on the throne. And he hasn't come down since."

Stir Crazy with Gene Wilder.

Silver Streak.

Reverend Rich in *Car Wash*.

Zeke in *Blue Collar*.

Stir Crazy.

Playing G.O.D., *In God We Trust*.

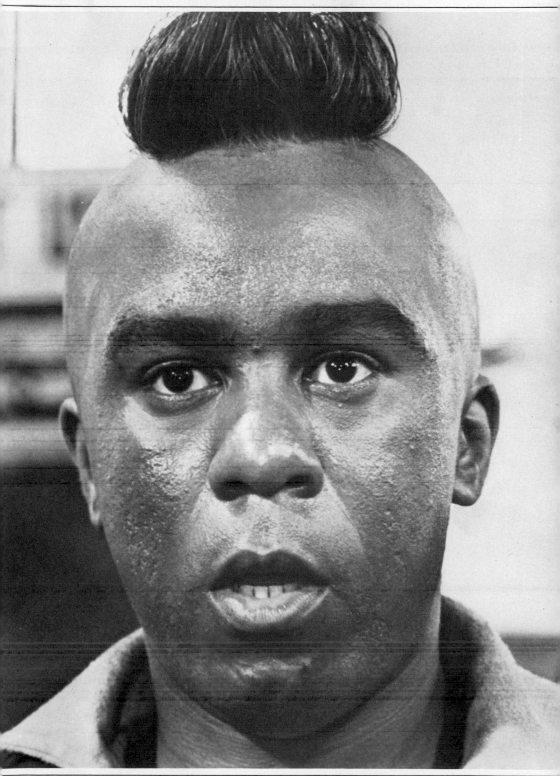

As Charlie Snow in *The Bingo Long Traveling All-Stars and Motor Kings*, he's a ball-player who tries to pass himself off as a Cuban and then as an Indian.

Which Way Is Up? Pryor played Leroy, a farm worker, Rufus, the worker's father, and the Rev. Lennox Thomas.

With her encouragement, he became a regular in future productions at the Center and, more importantly, began to emcee all their amateur talent contests.

Reminiscing recently about her discovery, Miss Whittaker said, like a doting parent, "Richard was a gifted child. If he had not come under the influence of the theater, I think he would have missed what he wanted most in life."

Juliette Whittaker and Pryor are in regular contact by phone and exchange visits. She has appeared with him on television, on *The Mike Douglas Show*. And, in addition to his scholarships at The Learning Tree—"Richard's commitment to the children of Peoria"—while making *Bustin' Loose*, he flew Miss Whittaker out to the Seattle filming site and asked her to bring some of her students to play minor roles in the movie.

Lily Tomlin, whose TV specials won Pryor his Emmy for Juliette Whittaker, said, "Of all the actors working now, he is the one who has the most instant rapport with his audience."

To David Felton, she elaborated, "To me, Richard is separate from anybody else. See, when I think of Richard, like the hours I've spent with him, and I see him improvise and tell me about his life, or people he's known, or whatever impressions he's had . . . it's like . . . so *uplifting*. Just because of his interpretation of it, and in the way he's perceived it . . . *humanistically*, you know, and then he himself, the fact that he exists . . . totally, like, just *uplifts* me. . . . It's like believing that we're all worth something, you know, when everything around us tells us that we're not really."

Actresses who have worked with Richard Pryor in movies speak of him in equally glowing terms.

Because of their torrid onscreen affair in *Some Kind of Hero*, certain tabloids speculated that Margot Kidder and Pryor, neither of them married at the time, were playing love scenes offscreen as well.

"I adore Richard but we weren't having an affair," said the actress. "I found it wonderful working with him. I kept waiting for him to turn into 'the lunatic.' But he never did. He is an extraordinarily serious and dramatic actor and a warm and special person. What makes Richard special is that he's the most real human being in the world. You could feel comfortable picking your toenails and eating them in front of him. He is just all-knowing about the human condition. He turned out to be even better than I'd hoped. He has that reality, that truth, that life force that is inextinguishable. He's full of power and wisdom. I love him very much and I was devastated when the filming was over."

Echoing these sentiments is the immortal Lena Horne, who appeared with Richard Pryor in *The Wiz*.

"I think he's marvelous, I love him," she says. "He is extremely clever and I wouldn't presume to say I understand what makes him tick, but whatever it is, I'm glad. I identify with Richard Pryor completely. I know everything he's talking about."

Discussing his comedy, Lena Horne says, "Though he's different, of course, he reminds me of Jonathan Winters. When he first started on TV they didn't know what the heck to do with him. Jonathan Winters was very fey, very out of some other planet, and people were not ready for somebody whose imagination just couldn't stand the realistic thing. He wanted to get to somewhere where it was so crazy that you could really absorb how crazy we act as a world anyway. You read the papers, we *are* insane. His insanity was so much more delicate than the real thing that nobody knew how to deal with it. And Richard, when he first started, was blowing people's minds. Not mine. I knew what he was doing. But they'd say, 'Now, what *is* this?' He opened in Las Vegas and they let him go and said, don't come back, and all that kind of nonsense."

What of his use of scatalogical language?

"I don't hear it, really. I suppose some black people get offended by it, but it doesn't offend me because, you see, I was raised around people who talked like that all the time. When I was sent away from my grandmother, I lived with my dad a couple of times above a joint he used to run, and the language Richard uses is pretty, compared to what I was hearing. So none of it shocks me."

She also has her own view as to why Pryor repetitiously employs the word "nigger" in his comedy.

"I think he does it," she says, "because it shocks all the people who aren't honestly really liberal. These people say, 'How dare he say that when I've tried my best to be liberal and not say it myself.' He forces them to take another look at themselves. So it's kind of infrastab.

"Comedy, like music, has changed. Richard Pryor's a new wave sort of person. When I hear people not of my own color use the same words, they don't use it with nearly the comfort or ease that Richard does. And until everybody says those words the same way, I think there's always going to be objection to Richard. But what he's talking about is universal comedy. It's so real, that's what's funny about it.

"The other thing is, he's selling tickets. If he wasn't, he would be dead. It's the same with all of us. If we weren't producing, we wouldn't be working. Richard, I think, will be around for a very long time because, basically, he's a great, great man."

Unlike Lena Horne, who had no scenes with Pryor in *The Wiz*, the beautiful Cicely Tyson, who was nominated for a Best Actress Oscar in *Sounder*, acted with him for weeks as his leading lady and love interest in *Bustin' Loose*.

What is it like, as a trained performer, to work so intimately over a long period of time with Richard Pryor, an instinctive, untutored actor?

"Oh boy, did we have a time at the beginning!" Cicely Tyson laughs. "When we first started shooting I did what I always do as an actress. I came in with my script prepared. But that was just the first couple of days. I would say a line and he would come up with something new, something not in the script. Then he would come to me and say, 'Listen, I'm awfully sorry, but tomorrow I'm gonna learn my lines and I'm gonna do it right.' Well, after the third day I said, 'Richard, just do whatever it is you feel you have to do. And I will just roll with the punches.' I mean, because he is an actor who works creatively out of himself. Plus he did write the script, and if he decided he wanted to change it, he certainly had the prerogative to do so. Normally I try as an actress to stick as closely to the script as possible, because that's what gives me the framework within which to function. In this case, I learned to react to whatever it was that he was doing."

Cicely Tyson admits that she approached *Bustin' Loose*, and Richard Pryor, with caution.

She says, "My lawyer and manager, David Franklin [who was also Pryor's lawyer at the time], came to me very apprehensively and said, 'Richard has this movie and he would like you to do it with him. And he doesn't think you would do it.' I said, 'Well, let me see the script first, then I'll make a decision.' After I'd read it I told David I would like to see Richard in person. Though I had never met him, and had never seen him in person even, I've always been a Richard Pryor fan. I've been with him from the days when he first appeared on Merv Griffin's show.

"At the time, he was doing *Richard Pryor in Concert*, so I flew to Atlanta to see him. I sat there, watching him perform, wondering, what exactly is it about him?

"I did not find what I expected. I wasn't offended by his

material, and I questioned myself as to why not. As I delved deeply into what was going on with that person on stage, I realized that he could say almost anything and not be offensive. It was as though it were a little child up there on stage who had just learned a few bad words and almost didn't know the meaning of them, but was saying them, really, for shock value. That was what I got. Plus the depth of his soul. That struck me. And that was what made me agree to do the movie."

Pryor has managed to break the boundaries of what is socially acceptable as comedy, and take it to its furthest advanced point, Cicely Tyson feels, "because his comedy is very open, and very honest, and very human. That's what makes all people identify with him in some way or other. He can make you laugh and cry at the same time. But if you were to ask him how he does this, I don't think he would be able to tell you. That is something intangible, what you call genius."

Do any black people resent him?

"At the very beginning," she replies, "there was a lot of resentment among blacks over the kinds of films he was doing. Yes, there was, quite a bit of resentment. I think that Richard became acutely aware of it and suddenly realized, himself, what it was that people were condemning him for. And that was one of the reasons he decided to do *Bustin' Loose*. He wanted to make a more positive contribution to blacks as a whole, and to the industry."

Yet, Cicely Tyson says, she understands Pryor's motives for making some of those early pictures which caused resentment.

"Sometimes," she explains, "a scream of any kind is done to get attention. Once the attention is focused on you, then you can speak. I think that's what Richard did. Scream. Now he's speaking."

In his comedy routines Richard Pryor repeatedly cites problems he had or witnessed as a kid that whites are responsible for, and conditions existing in the country today for which the government – still white-dominated – is accountable.

"I'm not of the opinion that he does this to make white people feel guilty, though," insists Cicely Tyson. "There are many ways in which one waves a banner. I choose to do it through the projects that I've done. I hope to make people aware of only one thing, that we blacks are human beings, no different. We eat, smell, see, taste, hear, feel, just like anyone else. The fact that our covering is of another hue does not make us any less human. Basically, that's what we're all trying to say. We want simply to be treated as human beings. That's all. I would venture to say that Richard's choice of banner waving has been no different from mine. Just to make people aware. I certainly did not set out in any of my projects to make people feel guilt. Sometimes that can turn into bitterness. The desired goal is just to make people *aware*."

Expressing her belief that Richard Pryor's future "has no limit; he can do almost anything he wants to do," Cicely Tyson sums up this way the secret of his universal, ever expanding popularity:

"If you know anything about Richard Pryor, you are able to see through to the core of the man. That's what reaches people, no matter what seems to be on the surface, no matter what the facade is. If you are sensitive at all, you know what's inside of the man. That's the attraction, that's what people perceive. What I see, and what I believe his audience sees, is a very vulnerable, super-sensitive, beautiful human being."

After producing Pryor's *Some Kind of Hero*, Hollywood's Howard Koch reports, from firsthand observation, "Women chase him all over. He is an attractive man, a lovely guy, you know. I just think he attracts women like flies. Women come from every direction. If we'd opened the doors of the studio we would have had thousands of them there."

Well aware of the roles so many women have played in his life, the great majority of them benevolent or beneficial, Richard Pryor said, "I like to share feelings with women. I really enjoy that. They're different from men, a lot different."

And that difference has made all the difference.

7.

*He whose word and deed you cannot predict, who answers
you without any supplication in his eyes, who draws his
determination from within, and draws it instantly – that
man rules.*

– Emerson

SOMETIMES IT HAS SEEMED THAT RICHARD
Pryor rules not only by unpredictability, but by living out his
most famous line from *Stir Crazy*: "You gotta be baaaad. Walk
baaaad, talk baaaad, look baaaad and nobody's gonna hassle
you."

Before the fire – and evidence indicates Pryor's a vastly
changed man since – William Brashler wrote in *Playboy*: "Being
around Pryor, say those who have experienced it, is like sleeping
in the company of a viper, of a presence that will slither lovingly
next to your skin as you breathe, gently caressing your eyelids,
hurting you not at all – then suddenly strike and cut you as
nobody and nothing has before."

Also prior to the fire, *Ebony*, commenting on the "image
that persists that he is a mercurial personality who might blow
his cool at any moment," added, "It is not a totally false image."

Newsweek observed in 1977: "Richard Pryor gives off an
aura of danger: it's both his sword and shield. Most people who
know him are afraid of him."

And a friend told *People* magazine in 1978: "Richard is
about eighty percent pure gold. The other twenty percent. well,
look out."

Thass Right, Thass Right, He Bad; Thass Right, Thass Right, He Good

Recorded events—all historical now—bear out the contention that he is, or was, a walking powderkeg with a very short fuse:

He once set a girlfriend's mink coat on fire after a fight.

He spent thirty-five days in a Pittsburgh jail after being convicted on an assault-and-battery charge brought by a girlfriend.

He broke the leg of one of his wives, resulting in an $1800 medical claim.

He has been sued for wife-beating.

In 1967 he beat up a Hollywood Sunset Strip motel clerk, was fined $300, put on probation, and paid an uncontested $75,000 claim.

He has been accused of stabbing a landlord with a fork.

He stabbed a soldier in the Army in Germany.

He punched an actor on the set of one of his movies who, soon after they had been introduced, invited him to his quarters by making what's been termed a "vulgar suggestion."

He was convicted of marijuana possession in San Diego and placed on probation for the misdemeanor offense.

Making *Blue Collar*, he engaged in fist fights with both his co-stars, Harvey Keitel and Yaphet Kotto.

Also on the *Blue Collar* set, actor George Memmoli charged that Pryor hit him over the head with a chair, fracturing his skull; Memmoli filed suit for one million dollars.

He was arrested after that New Year's Day 1978 car-smashing episode involving his then wife, Deboragh McGuire, and two friends of hers, Beverly Clayborn, twenty-five, and Edna Solomon, thirty-seven. According to L.A. detective Lewis Bobbitt, "Witnesses said the three women were ejected from the house by force, chased around the yard in a car by Pryor and shot at when they escaped into the street." Witnesses also said Pryor "rammed the victims' car with his Mercedes Benz five or six times," Bobbitt added. The denouement: the assault with a deadly weapon charge, a felony, was dropped for lack of sufficient evidence. But he was ordered not to possess guns or other deadly weapons during his probation period. After a plea of no contest to the charge that he had rammed his car into the other vehicle, a misdemeanor offense, the Superior Court in Van Nuys ordered him to donate his services for ten benefit performances for a worthy cause or face four months in jail. He was also told to seek psychiatric care and to pay restitution to Edna Solomon and Beverly Clayborn.

In her divorce suit against Pryor, filed one month after this fracas, Deboragh McGuire Pryor asked the court to restrain the comedian from "annoying, threatening or harassing" her.

In September 1977, he made headlines again when he was a guest star at a benefit for the Gay Liberation Movement at the Hollywood Bowl. At the microphone, addressing the crowd of

17,000 predominantly gay whites, he launched into an obscenity-laced 15-minute diatribe. He lambasted them for "cruising" Hollywood Boulevard "when the niggers was burnin' down Watts." Before exiting the stage, he taunted them with his now-famous farewell line: "Kiss my happy rich black ass" – delivered with an appropriate gesture (dropping his pants and flipping his bird at them).

His angry query to the Bowl crowd, "Where were you when Watts was burning?", was rhetorical. And it brought this bemused response from his manager: "Well, I know where he was. He was at my house watching it on television." But it is also well known that Pryor opened his heart to benefit blacks in poverty-stricken Watts at a 1972 concert in the Los Angeles Coliseum.

Despite the brouhaha that followed the Hollywood Bowl incident, he later insisted he had no regrets. "Life must go on," he said, closing that chapter. "You pay your dues and take what comes."

There was more to that "Kiss my happy rich black ass" story than has ever been told. According to Michael Schultz, his *Greased Lightning* director, who was there, Pryor's outburst on stage was totally justified.

Says Schultz: "Richard, who is probably one of the most sensitive people I've ever met, came to that concert to donate his time freely to the cause of the Gay Rights Movement. But what he saw backstage was blatant racism. That is what set him off. There were two groups of dancers backstage, one black and one white. And the manager, the guy who was running the whole thing – somebody connected with Bette Midler – was definitely giving the black group second-class treatment and talking offensively to them. It really flipped Richard out. There he was, willing to go out on the line for people who were being discriminated against, and, backstage, he was witnessing another kind of discrimination, racial discrimination.

"He had been drinking quite heavily, and enough not to hide his own personal hurt at seeing people being discriminated against. When he came out on the stage he was visibly disturbed. The hypocrisy of it all provoked his unexpected behaviour that night. Anybody else would have stuffed it and tried to rationalize it. But he came out on that stage in front of 17,000 people and told them how upset he was and exactly what was on his mind. He criticized the lying under the banner of being openly free. Though he made general statements, he was striking at the duality of professing one thing and practicing another. He wasn't accusing the entire audience. But he was saying, 'A lot of you people are full of shit. A lot of you who are here are still not out of the closet – with *everything*, with your entire self, not just your profession of being gay.' And that's what *really* happened at the Hollywood Bowl."

Of the many other imbroglios in his past, Richard Pryor has offered this blanket explanation: "Every time I get in trouble, it's because I end up drinking too much, or I end up snorting too much, or smoking too much."

Sometimes he has merely been mischievous. Like the time he was a spectator in a nightclub when the star attraction, a lady singer, long overstayed her welcome on the stage. Tearing his hair, the club's manager implored somebody to do something. Recalls one witness: "Richard Pryor did. He sauntered cross-stage to the warbling female, who wondered why her audience was suddenly rolling on the floor and screaming – until she noticed that Pryor was wearing nothing but a tie."

Other times, bad business judgment has plunged him into deep hot water. The prime example of this is when he neglected to file federal income tax returns on $250,000 earned from 1967 to 1970. Indicted on four evasion counts, he plea bargained and was fined twenty-five hundred dollars and sentenced to ten days in Los Angeles County jail. "I wasn't embarrassed," he said later. "I was bitter. Every day I thought the judge was going to come down and apologize and let my ass out of there. But I must say, I was glad it wasn't eleven days." On his last day in "stir," incidentally, he put on an impromptu show for his fellow inmates and won a standing ovation.

Around NBC, you can still feel the bad vibes whenever Richard Pryor's name is mentioned – because of *The Richard Pryor Show,* which was aborted after the network aired four episodes in the fall of 1977.

Trouble began immediately with the opening skit of the first show. In this segment, Pryor, appearing nude from the waist up, denied he made compromises to get his act on television, adding, "I've given up absolutely nothing." The camera then pulled back to show him naked except for a flesh-colored body stocking that gave the impression he'd been emasculated. To his chagrin, NBC, which had promised him artistic freedom, snipped the scene.

Siding with the comedian, one critic observed: "Maybe if NBC hired Farrah Fawcett-Majors they'd ask her to cut her hair. Maybe they'd give Nureyev a desk job. Maybe if they reunited

The Beatles it would be on condition that they promise not to sing. It makes as much sense as giving Richard Pryor a prime-time hour of comedy and then expecting him to be safe, sane and squeaky-clean."

"They retained about six thousand people to do nothing but mess with my material," Pryor said of NBC's censors. "A lot of the people who control the television medium are fascists. They have one-track minds when it comes to creative thinking. It bothers me that one person's judgment [the censor's] is better than the creative people who put it together."

Actually, in the weeks before the show went on the air, Pryor had sent up warning signals of trouble ahead. To his staff of TV comedy writers, according to *Newsweek*'s Maureen Orth, he confided: "You know something? I don't *want* to be on TV. I'm in a trap. I can't do this – there ain't no art. . . . I bit off more than I can chew. I was turning into a greedy person. They give you so much money you can't refuse." When one of the writers reminded him that he had the chance to do something different on TV, he said, "You want to see me with my brains blown out? . . . I'm not stable enough. I don't want to drink and I don't want to snort and I can't do it no other way."

He and NBC settled their differences in a manner greatly to his financial benefit. They would pay him two million dollars *not* to appear on any other network for five years while doing six specials at irregular intervals for them. He declared at the time: "I'm going to do them the way I want to and then they can kiss my behind."

He still harbors no affection for today's commercial television, saying, "Basic truths are not told on TV, which 127 million people watch every night. It's just used for commercials to keep people working so that they have to go to the loan companies for money to buy products. They brainwash you, man, it's a bunch of bullshit, it's evil. The top-rated shows are for retarded people. They're not going to write shows about how to revolutionize America. But it could be such an informative medium. One week of truth on TV could just straighten out everything."

All mistakes and unfortunate headlines to the contrary, there is a flip side to the Richard Pryor coin, which has a bright and shining gleam.

"He is the softest touch in town," says Deboragh McGuire Pryor, who still speaks fondly of him despite their divorce. "He'll loan money to anyone and never care if or when it's paid back."

Says magazine writer Sue Reilly: "Money's not a hangup for Pryor—he's made a name for well-meaning, if slightly fulsome, charity. He will send a helpful secretary not a bouquet of flowers but an entire truckload; he gave individual Christmas presents to all twenty messengers at Universal. A diamond-studded pinkie ring went to his record producer, a gold bracelet to an old friend."

Typical of his gift-giving is the expensive watch he bought for June Eckstine, a long-time friend, when she helped him find the palatial house he bought in Northridge.

These are examples of his learning to give only to those he *wants* to give to, which he learned the hard way.

"When I first got a break and was on television," he has said, "I went back to Peoria for one thing: *acceptance*. I just wanted to be accepted by the people who had told me I wasn't shit. I thought I could get their acceptance by offering them money, because that's what they really wanted. . . . This is hard, but it's got to be said. I couldn't relate to my family. Only cash related. It seemed that they liked me for that only. Later on, I felt that I didn't have anyone that I could just pick up the phone and talk to in the middle of the night unless I was calling to say I was sending some money."

Over the years, he has bought homes and cars for relatives. Unfortunately, he has not always been rewarded for his generosity.

An actor friend, Leonard Gaines, reports, "When Richard was in the hospital after the fire, people close to him who were supposed to be saving him was robbing him—robbing the shit out of him."

Pryor confirmed this to *Ebony*, saying, with tears in his eyes, "Man, like even when I was in the hospital fighting for my life, there were people close to me, people I trusted, members of my own family [he did not mean his children], here in my house deciding what they were going to have. My watches are missing. My money is missing. Some of my jewelry is gone. But I fooled them. I'm alive, and now they have to give all that shit back."

While all this was going on, Pryor, forgetting his own pain, was lending support and encouragement to fellow patients in his hospital burn ward.

Said the Sherman Oaks Community Hospital spokesman, Gary Swaye, "Pryor knows the names of all twenty of the other burn patients, adults and children, whom he meets in therapy and elsewhere in the Center. He has been friendly to them and has encouraged them. He says it is a mutual admiration society because they are all for his recovery, too."

While still at the Center fighting for his life, the actor established the Richard Pryor Burn Foundation, designed to raise funds for medical research and to help burn victims cover treatment costs. It was kicked off with a fourteen-hour telethon emceed by actor Leon Isaac Kennedy and Altovise Davis (Sammy Davis Jr.'s wife), which Pryor watched from his hospital bed. It garnered $140,000 in pledges from viewers.

For years he has given generously to the cause of medical research – $100,000 to Jerry Lewis' Muscular Dystrophy Fund, another $100,000 to the Charles R. Drew Post Graduate Medical School, among others – saying, "I gotta do something for the money they pay me."

Late in 1981, surprisingly, he headlined a comic group at Hollywood's Comedy Store to benefit the John Wayne Clinic at UCLA via the Committee to Cure Cancer Through Immunization. Surprisingly, because John Wayne was known for his extreme right-wing political views, and, Pryor has said, "John Wayne hated me" – meaning black people.

Prisoners and convicts, as individuals and groups, have long enjoyed his empathy and support. Once when he gave a benefit performance at the Lorton Correctional Complex in Virginia, he was impressed by a singing group of inmates, the Inner Voices. He invited them to appear with him at the Apollo and arranged for them to do so. When the Inner Voices returned to Lorton, it was with the roar of life-sustaining applause echoing in their ears. Apollo audiences had told them something they had almost forgotten – they were *worth* something.

Pryor is also a contributing friend of the Fortune Society, spearheaded by the Kennedy clan, which aids ex-convicts and presents annual awards to former prisoners now making their mark in the outside world.

After the fire, when he was in New York to promote *Stir Crazy*, Pryor reserved time to personally meet the members of the Fortune Society. He talked to the ex-offenders about drugs, urging them to abstain. Although he had once said he would never preach to anyone; he addressed them from personal experience. "I used to smoke base but that stuff will kill you. Dope is for dopes. What is good is getting high on energy. I get high on myself now and I really like Richard." He talked to them about the criminal justice system and encouraged them to become achievers, reminding them realistically, "If you have money, you can get out of anything but if you don't have money, you're at the mercy of the court. It's tough." Afterwards he told reporter Ernie Johnston Jr. that he had learned something from the session. "I have a lot to say now. I went through something that I hope every human being won't have to go through. But it's very hard to tell young people because they haven't done it." Still he keeps trying.

Early in the summer of 1981, he played peacemaker in the long-running feud among thirty street gangs in the crime-infested areas of Watts, Compton, Inglewood and other South Central sections of Los Angeles. He told gang members he would put up $200,000 of his own money if they would help stop the violence in their neighborhoods. His financial contribution went into a self-help education program administered by the Sheenway School in Watts. It worked. The crime rate during the hot summer months went down drastically.

He never loses sight of people as individuals who may be in need of a helping hand. One Pryor intimate tells of a woman friend of the comic's, the owner of a failing club who "was dead on her ass, busted out broke." When Pryor learned of her dire financial condition, he performed nightly at her club, gratis, to SRO audiences, until she was back on her feet again. And when singer Jackie Wilson collapsed and lay in a hospital in a coma, Pryor donated a large chunk of the earnings from one of his albums to Wilson's young children.

Blacks, understandably, remain central in the focus of Richard Pryor's moral, financial and professional commitment. Both spiritually and financially, he is a major contributor to black charities. Making certain that members of the local branch of the NAACP were able to attend when *Roots* author Alex Haley lectured in Los Angeles, he purchased and donated one thousand tickets. And, above all else, he has dedicated himself, heart and soul, to creating, via motion pictures, a positive image of blacks in America.

Richard the Good has more than balanced the scales.

8.

THE PEOPLE WHO KNOW RICHARD PRYOR BEST are his fellow comedians – they've studied the man and his humor and know where he's coming from – and those who have worked with him and have observed him intimately at close range.

In search of the "real" Richard Pryor, let's go tape-to-type and see what they have to reveal about him.

HOWARD W. KOCH
(Producer of Some Kind of Hero*)*

"Richard is one of the greatest performers of our time. So Chaplinesque. He can make you laugh or cry in the same sentence. I didn't know him really well until we did *Some Kind of Hero*. But I had met him many years ago when I was head of the studio here at Paramount, and we did a picture called *The Busy Body*. It was Richard's first film. And hell, he was just glad he was living, you know. I didn't meet him again till he got in trouble with a shooting. He tried to shoot his wife, or maybe it was her car. I wrote a letter to the probation officer. We got friendly again that way. Then finally, all of a sudden, we made *Some Kind of Hero* together. This was one of the great experiences. I loved it. Of course, I'd heard about his 'explosive unpredictability.' So I was waiting for that. I always felt that from when I knew him before. And I was waiting for that explosive hate that might come out. But that never showed. He couldn't have been nicer, more cooperative. He's a great guy. I just fell in love with him. He was a doll and I'm not just bullshitting. Everybody was crazy about him – the whole crew, the actors and actresses, electricians, my secretary. And he is so compassionate of others. We had one bad moment when one of our actors got a little broken up [implying a drug problem]. And Richard was really devastated over it, because he was trying to reach this guy and tell him how bad it was. He couldn't, you know. But Richard was really torn apart by that because he had lived through it. And he is so marvelously inventive as an actor. One day we had a simple scene – just showing him in a prison cell while it was raining.

Friends and Others

Then, ad-libbing, he started singing *Queen of the Nile*. It was hilarious and we got it on film. That's his ability to come on with something in the middle of nothing and, all of a sudden, turn it into a tremendous thing. I just know that if he stays healthy, which I'm sure he will, and doesn't get his emotional life too screwed up, which I hope he won't, there's no telling how far he can go."

MICHAEL PRESSMAN
(Director of Some Kind of Hero*)*

"Richard is considered one of the few geniuses around today. He is the best actor I've ever worked with – free, open to suggestions, conceptual and incredibly talented. He embellishes each scene with his rare touch and has embraced this film and his role with total dedication."

BUDD FRIEDMAN
(Owner of The Improv, where Pryor worked as a young comedian in New York)

"He's brilliant, no doubt about that, and I could tell it from the start. But we've had an up-and-down relationship. Here's a classic story. He came in the club one night and was very hostile. Up until that time we'd gotten along just great. No problems. And my ex-wife – my wife at the time – adored him too. I was at the club alone and he came in – it was one of the few times he was with a black woman – and he gives me some bullshit that I take advantage of him because he's black. I was really devastated. I got home and I told my wife this, and she said, 'Oh, you should have told him you take advantage of all performers, regardless of race, color or creed!' It's become one of my standard jokes. Then six months later – I hadn't seen him for about four or five months – he came back to the club and hugged me, and everything was just fine. It was just his way of reacting that night, I guess.

"A good story about the night he came back: he and I went out to breakfast. About four in the morning, we were on

Second Avenue trying to get a cab to the West Side. He was staying at the Henry Hudson Hotel and I lived in the West Seventies. We split a cab; in those days you couldn't get a cab in New York. So this cab goes by off-duty. Richard yells and whistles in the street after him. The cab stops, backs up, and the guy – a young black driver – says, 'Come on, get in.' And this kid says to Richard, 'Let me ask you one question. How come you never show up for *The Ed Sullivan*?' And Richard, who'd missed a performance or two, says, 'Well, I sleep late.' So I said, 'It's a good thing he recognized you, Richard, otherwise we'd never have gotten a ride.' And the cab driver says, 'Oh no, it's *you* I recognized, Budd; I've only seen Richard at your club besides on television.' So he recognized *me*. Richard and I both fell on the floor. I mean, you want to talk about deflating the balloon! But that goes a long way back. I really haven't spoken more than four words to him in the last five or six years. As for Richard's future, I think he's got to mellow or die. I mean if he continues to be successful. He'll mellow; success usually has that effect."

CICELY TYSON
(Pryor's co-star in Bustin' Loose*)*

"Yes, I've heard the stories that he 'might explode at any moment.' But I think that is true of anyone who's lived on the periphery, whose nerve ends are so raw and sensitized that if you touch them they will explode. And that's the way Richard is. There are moments when he seems totally introverted, and for the most part he is. He's a person who lives very deep. Within himself. His mind is constantly going. You can look at him and see the turmoil within him. He's very scrupulous about his work. And this makes him, as with any sensitive artist, frightened, wanting desperately to do the right thing, and questioning from time to time whether it is. This was all very obvious to me. Before the accident he was very loose and funny. He was always kidding around with everyone on the set. Children loved him, the crew. He had this very strong need to keep everyone up. After the accident he was the other way. He would talk to people, but he did not go to the extremes that he did before the accident. He would come out and shoot his scenes, and then he would go back into his dressing room. It was very wearing for him. He had recovered in a much shorter period than they expected, and I think it took a lot out of him to come back to work that soon."

PAUL SCHRADER
(Director of Blue Collar*)*

"I have a very strong and probably strained affection for him. The man is the most conflicted, tortured personality I have ever met. *Blue Collar* – my first film – was certainly the most difficult film experience I've had, and, I suspect, that I'll ever have. I didn't realize how excruciating it was until I started directing other films. But when I finished it I told myself that, if this is what directing was, I didn't want to do it. It was just too grueling. On the set, it would be a physical fight or abusive language. Richard was insulting people. What I call the 'pendulum effect' is very strong in him. If he was really nice one day, and people were nice to him, you could expect a rough day the next. If he was really rough one day and vicious to people – insulting and abusive – you could pretty well expect the next day he was going to go around and patch everything up. My job on *Blue Collar*, in which we were dealing with dramatic and racially controversial material, was not to let up on the pressure. There were three actors who were at approximately the same stage in their career – Harvey Keitel, Yaphet Kotto and Richard Pryor. And they were all determined to assert themselves in this movie. It was like putting three bulls in a china shop and making sure that none of them got out. My job was just to keep them working, keep them equal, and under pressure. And each one misinterpreted my efforts as favoring another of the three. Richard was convinced he was being played as the black sidekick to the white hero. Harvey Keitel was convinced that he was being played as the white straight man to the black comic. Yaphet Kotto was convinced that he was the second-class black to both of them. And each one of them, every day, tried to hold his ground and protect his territory. So tension was everpresent. And it would come down to arguments over improvisations and negotiations over words. Toward the end no one was speaking. It was very tense. But it was a situation that I – not they – had created. I had picked these three personalities and put them in this material and that auto-plant setting. And this was the result. I didn't purposely create that tension. I created it by the packaging, and once the packaging was over, I tried my best to keep things smooth. Richard said to me that he didn't want black audiences to come to *Blue Collar* unprepared and be devastated at seeing him in the kind of role they didn't expect. He said he was worried about rejection and didn't think he could stand it. I didn't put much credence by that. I wasn't sympathetic. He was thinking of himself as a personality rather than an actor. I said, 'Look, you want to be an actor, you be an actor, you play a character. If you want to be a public personality, that's another decision, and you shouldn't be doing this movie.' But he had not yet straightened out in his mind, if he has now, the difference between being a public figure and being an actor.

"Richard's an enigma in that he's totally tortured by inherent contradictions in his personality. He is uniquely gifted in that he can be simultaneously both big and black, to an extent that no other entertainer has been able to be. He can be big, very successful across the board: white and black communities, lower class, upper class, middle class. He can also be extremely black, which means very, very parochial, very ethnic and inside the black community humor. Very few black entertainers have been given this gift. They either work from the streets or they work in the middle class genre. But they don't try both. Richie, because of that boyish, disingenuous quality of his, can work both sides of the street. But what happens is that the bigger he gets, the more successful he is in the white world, the more resentful he becomes, the more afraid that he's not being black enough. Whereupon he will do something very pathological and very dramatic, to remind everyone that he is black first and big second. The moment people start to be too nice to him – I mean white people, and they can be a little too condescending – the clock starts ticking and it's just a matter of time before he's going to blow. And the moment he blows, does something really offensive to the middle class constituency, he is immediately struck with remorse, and fearful that he's no longer going to be big, that he's only going to be black. So then you see the pendulum swinging dramatically in the other direction. He will do something to ingratiate himself into the mainstream, into the white audience. That just starts the other process going. The more he ingratiates himself – giving gifts, starting conversations, treating people with concern – the nicer he gets to others and the nicer they are to him, the more he starts to get afraid that he isn't being black anymore. You never know quite what he will do at any given time. There are certain trigger buttons. When you see somebody push one of them around him, you know he's going to blow. But it's never quite predictable. And the extremes of the pendulum can be quite surprising. His extreme anger and abusiveness and cruelty can be a real shocker. But his ass-kissing can be equally shocking. When he hits either end of the swing, you really do get taken aback. You say, 'Oh my God!' This agony of his, deriving from the fact that he's both big and black, seems to make it impossible for him to find some compromise between being both. But I haven't seen him in a long while. So maybe he has found some compromise.

"Don't ask what effect I think the accident has had, or will have, on him. I have no idea whatsoever. I mean, he could be a changed man, or the contradictions may be so deep that they will just lie dormant for a while. You're talking about a man who has had to survive this personal conflict through drugs and alcohol, just to kill the pain. Now if he's found another way to kill the pain and to integrate himself, through some kind of therapy or religious commitment, etc., he may be in good shape. But if he hasn't, it will have to be a return to the old crutches and it will all start over again. I get a call from him every now and again, but, somehow, the whole drama starts to get reenacted, you know? Well, really, I don't work for anybody and it's pretty hard for someone like me to be that close to Richard. Because I have my own demons and my own concerns. And he is not high on my priority of concerns. He needs people around him who are very, very interested in him, and that's not my job, that's not my life. Yes, I would like to work with him again, but it's a matter of who plays the fiddle and who does the jig."

DAN AYKROYD
(Comedy star)

"People love to hear the truth reinterpreted and represented in a way they haven't heard before. And Richard Pryor speaks the truth. He speaks from true wells within himself and from the truth of the human experience in the 1980s. He touches so many neurons with what he says simply because everything he speaks rings of actual human experience. That's what makes him exciting and really successful. I think if he stays this raw and sensitive to what's happening he'll be able to do it until he's sixty and beyond. Can a man still think as funny after a traumatic experience like the fire? I think a funny man can. If you're born with it, if it's in the chemistry, in the blood, no matter what happens you're going to try to see the worst possible world situation as a humorous one. You're going to try to find something to laugh about in it, just because of your basic nature. Now this is the type of human being that Richard Pryor is. He just has always been a satirist, a wit, a caustic. This is the way his mind and soul work. So no matter what he's going to go through in life, he'll try to first conquer that problem, that fear, and then turn around and try to find humor and warmth and comedy in it somehow."

LEONARD GAINES
(Actor–Restaurateur–Boxing promoter–Producer)

"Is he a new man now? A new man as far as being an actor is concerned? Yeah. Probably. . . part-time on the job and everything else. Has he really been reborn? I don't know about that. Sometimes he's good natured, sometimes he's not . . . he's a changeable guy. Making *Blue Collar* (in which Gaines played the benign Internal Revenue Service investigator) got him uptight. He had fights, but he was very nice to me when we worked together. Anyway, he wasn't too funny while making that picture. 'Cause it was a serious picture.

"Now? Since the fire? I didn't know if he could be the fucking same funny guy or not anymore. When there's a tragedy like that, I didn't think he could be as loose and funny as he was, you know. I didn't think his funnybone would be there now. Like when he was free and ad libbing and really wild.

"Like he was on *This Nigger is Crazy*, you know. Is he still crazy? Personally, I thought he wouldn't be, because once you clean yourself up, you turn into something else. You'd be doing a different brand of comedy. You wouldn't be doing 'Fuck you, man,' 'Shit, man' and 'This fucking white chick moved out on me,' you know.

"You're trying to do a different kind of humor. Your observations are different, you're living in a different world. Richard was fucking bananas . . . shooting up his wife's car, doing this and that and yet coming out with fucking funny lines when he was real sick.

"And I wondered, when you're very well, what's so funny. . . you've got a different outlook on life. What can you do to break people up now? Think of that. I mean, what could Richard Pryor be thinking about if he's cleaned himself up and he's a different guy? And he's not looking toward the streets anymore? I wondered where would his humor come from, you know?

"But evidently I was wrong. 'Cause he just did that concert for Ray Stark and Columbia Pictures, which they filmed, and he was fucking sensational! So I guess his accident didn't have much effect as far as his funnybone is concerned.

"If you go through something traumatic, you would think that could happen to anybody, and as far as doing funny things, you would change. It's like Sid Caesar. I think his humor changed because he went through analysis for twenty years. He was a much funnier guy before he went under analysis.

"And Richard uses his accident in his act now. And gets big laughs! I guess that's what they mean by tragedy and comedy. You've got to have an awful lot of tragedy to get an awful lot of laughs. It really proves the guy is a genius because whatever tragedy he has gone through – and he's gone through an awful lot of it for the last twenty-five years – using all those tragic times in his life and turning them around and making laughs out of them is something to marvel at.

"I mean, all comedians make light of troubles, 'cause that's where tragedy and comedy come from, but Richard has a deeper insight into tragedy and can get more laughs out of it than another guy. Another comedian would do different kinds of jokes about burning up, not as heavy as Richard's. Richard's burn jokes would probably be better than any other comedian's burn jokes.

"But he's also a fucking great actor! Matter of fact he made me cry in *Lady Sings the Blues*. He brought tears to my eyes and I was a fan of his from then on.

"But I hope he keeps us laughing for the next forty years. I hope he doesn't have to suffer as much as he did, though."

SALLY HANSON
(Motion picture costume designer)

"Richie and I have been friends for many years. I think he's a genius. He can pick up an object and just go into hilarious routines. I remember one time, in one of those California heat waves where it stayed a hundred and four degrees, when seven or eight people gathered around my swimming pool. And he started in just doing Richie during the late afternoon and didn't stop until four-thirty in the morning. People had to go and lie down and rest because they were laughing so hard. They still talk about that evening. People ask where this well-spring of humor comes from. The answer is: pain. He had, you know, a really rough upbringing – such a painful childhood that the only survival was humor. It's a desperate kind of humor, but it's brilliant. And he's done some brilliant things that almost no one has ever seen. One was his performance in the movie *A Kind of Loving,* for which, incidentally, I did the clothes. It played about fourteen weeks in Paris but, I think, about two days in America. And that's a pity. He's one of the most brilliant minds I've ever come across. I've heard some say of him that he could 'explode at any moment.' But I think that's possible with anybody as greatly talented as Richie. That explosive quality is pretty basic with comedians, really successful ones. As for his scatological humor, I've always had great empathy for Richie, and maybe that's why the language has never bothered me. There are a lot worse things than bad words. And when he uses the word 'nigger,' it's not derogatory. Would he be offended if a white person used it? That would depend on who the white person was. If it was an offensive person, I'm sure he would be offended. But, from someone on his own level, a friend, using it in jocular terms, he would regard it as an endearment."

CARL REINER
(Comedy star–writer)

"Richard Pryor is looked up to by every other comedian as the ultimate artist, because he has had the courage to express himself 100 percent. Steve Martin and I—in fact every comedian I know—consider him an absolute genius."

CLEAVON LITTLE
(Stage-screen actor; star of Blazing Saddles*)*

"Pryor's comedy I find extremely funny. He's brilliant. I would like to see him write—do a lot of writing. I would love to act in whatever he would write. His kind of comedy I can identify with more closely than with Mel Brooks' kind, for obvious reasons. Mel's is Jewish and Richard's is black. He can become one of the great comic writers if he will only put it down in terms of a story—a play or a movie—where he's not doing it just for his own act, for himself, but for other actors to act in. That may be the next move for him. I think he can probably do it better than most people. Now I don't know what Richard is like now. I knew him about five years ago when I did *Greased Lightning* with him. Was he funny to be around? At times, yes. On occasion, when he felt like it, he'd just start talking and you'd laugh. He'd put you on the floor. I mean, you felt good in your laughter—you felt what he was talking about. Sometimes it was a horrible thing, but he would put a point of view on it that'd have you hysterical with laughter. He is not a predictable person at all. The one predictable thing about him is his unpredictability. You can predict he will not do the same thing twice. If he reads a line, he'll read it ten different ways. If you give him a minute, he'll come up with ten more. That's the truth about him as an artist, as a creative mind, creative spirit. Richard is a very moody person. He may want to talk and he may not. Once I walked up to him and put on an act like I was his biggest fan. I said, 'Hey, man, can I get your autograph?' And he was in one of his moods. He had his head dropped down. And he sort of looked up, like 'Don't bother me.' Then he really looked at me, and recognized me, and busted out laughing. And we talked.

"He's a man with a lot of feeling, a lot of things going on inside of him. So that will reflect itself at times in his mood. But I really don't know Richard that well. I remember an experience I had once with Richard – many years ago, after I met him – and he talked about something personal. It was very funny. As I listened, though, it touched something else that was in me that, as funny as it was, was also very sad to me. And I asked him some more questions. Then he got very upset, pissed off at me, and he said something which hurt me. I just, finally, had to leave the situation. In retrospect, though, that's what comedy is. It really is pain. When they say he's brilliant, I must say that's probably what it is. I never like to use that word too loosely, but he certainly is brilliant in being able to capture pain and, with a sense of love, make it laughter. I think he is a person who will go down in history in the world of entertainment as a great comedian and actor. He will last, he will be there. He is a natural survivor. Take what happened with *Blazing Saddles* – an ironic twist which is so funny. There was a time when Mel Brooks wanted Richard to play the sheriff, the part that I finally did. (That caused, for a certain period of time, a kind of chasm in our relationship.) The funniest thing was that Warner Bros. did not want Richard to do it because, they said, he was so crazy. But as time has gone by, with his records and movies like *Greased Lightning*, he's made millions of dollars off of Warner Bros. Which means it's a business."

MICHAEL SCHULTZ
(Director of Greased Lightning *and* Which Way Is Up?*)*

"When you meet Richard, when you are with him, he's very humble and charming. People are attracted to him. But, yes, some people are afraid of him in the sense that he will see right to the heart of the matter. And, if anybody is harboring a prejudice or hiding some kind of negative feelings, he has a sixth sense that knows exactly what that is, and he will lay it out in public. He will come out and tell everybody who's within earshot exactly what's on his mind, if he feels like it. So the people who are afraid of him are the people who are really afraid of being found out. But I don't think he's angry. I think that part of his act – humor based on anger – disappeared in the fire. He definitely is coming at life from a different point of view now."

DAVID BRENNER
(Comedy star)

"I'm a great fan of his, a great admirer of him. I think a lot of what Richie says is validated by truthful history. I mean, to different degrees, we *have* persecuted the black man since the first one stepped ashore. Maybe there's less of it today, but there's certainly been enormous persecution of the black up to now. And of other minorities. If we had a Puerto Rican comedian – we once had Freddie Prinze – or an American Indian comedian, you'd hear the same thing from them. It's better to have a minority group represented by a comedian than by a man who wears a ski mask and forms an underground terrorist group. And if Richard Pryor hits the conscience of those who are undecided whether to like or dislike blacks, and swings them over towards an episodic point of view, then he's serving a very great purpose for his people. And I approve of it entirely. Let's face it, the American black has fought wars for a country that did not give him first-class citizenship. And the most decorated infantry group in World War II was an all-black division, the most decorated fighter group in that war was a black flyer unit, and we don't recognize the black man. Richard Pryor's speaking out for blacks, and doing it at a time when it's needed, because we Americans are under pressure from the world. And we'd better pull ourselves together as a single group, and join hands here, because we're being pressured economically, and spiritually, and physically by a lot of the world. Richard is helping us get together. I don't think he is hostile toward whites in general. Because if you look at him, you see that he works, plays, hangs out with, and is friends with whites. He's not hostile toward whites on a one-to-one basis. What he's hostile toward, what his humor is hostile toward, is the whites who are hostile toward blacks. It's hostility vs. hostility. And its aim is to achieve a mutual understanding, a reconciliation, which is crucial at this particular time. A unified United States is top priority now. Look what's happening all over the world. They just blew up a synagogue in Belgium, and killed Jews because they were Jews. You can't deny that the Nazi party works out of Orange County in California. You can't ignore that the KKK is still active. I mean, you cannot pretend that there's no persecution in this country against minority groups. And if people speak out from a minority group, for that minority group, I said, God bless them."

BUCK HENRY
(Comic actor–screenwriter)

"The closer a comedian gets to a kind of truth, the tougher it is for a large part of the audience to accept what he does as comedy, but the stronger the hard core of his audience becomes. But Richard appeals to everybody now on some level or other. He can make a G-rated film or an X-rated film. He's very, very talented and flexible. I've tried to think of his equivalent in the white world, but I'm not sure that there is one. I'm not sure he's not the equivalent in the white world. If he's had any influence on white comics, I can't think of an example. But I'm sure there are a lot of guys in the Improvisations and Comedy Stores all over the country who are trying to use Richard's ability to take a cliché and turn it inside out, and apply that to the white world. God willing that they do, because it sure would be a great step from the gaggy, sort of second-rate joke telling that most of the young comics today are doing. As for Richard's use of street language, that's nothing new. It's been forever. The history of literature has been that, and of entertainment. I mean, Aristophanes was considered dirty. Rabelais was dirty, Mark Twain was dirty. Throughout the history of literature, which was where people were entertained before there was television and movies, the most advanced, the most original, the front leaders of those who wrote and made people laugh and think were often accused of being pornographic, scatalogical or obscene, or all three. Richard's growth has been revealing to me. I knew him very, very superficially early on. He was friends of friends of mine. What kind of guy he was, I don't really know. He just seemed to be kind of guarded, nice. I knew he was real funny, that's all. But I didn't know he was *that* funny. I relate to him because he makes me laugh. And there are no boundaries on his future. He can do whatever he wants to do. He's a certified motion picture star. He's one of three or four people who can guarantee an audience—more so than Burt Reynolds [a recently acquired friend of Pryor's], possibly more so than Barbra Streisand. I mean, Richard is incredible when you see what his name means to a film. He's going to be enormous. He's wealthy now. He's going to be enormously wealthy within a few years. He'll be able to do anything and everything he wants to do."

ROB COHEN
(Producer of The Bingo Long Traveling All-Stars and Motor Kings *and* The Wiz*)*

"When I first took up with Pryor he was at a very low point in his career. We wanted him for *Bingo Long* and he didn't want to do it. I went over to his house and talked him into it. I explained to him how important this picture was, because there was a section of black history, black baseball, that had never really been treated in film. We got along very well. He immediately understood that I was telling him the truth. He has an infallible truth detector, or lie detector. He was much angrier and much more radical than he is today. Once he read the screenplay he agreed to do it. When we were doing *Bingo* down in Georgia I saw the truly giving side of him. We were night-shooting in these little towns that hadn't changed much since the '30s. The black population would gather around, because they'd heard of Billy Dee Williams and James Earl Jones, and so on. But the one that everybody wanted to see was Pryor. He would stand out in the street and give a free impromptu concert, telling jokes, for hours – once till four or five in the morning. And they would get going into the black dialect so thick that, despite as much time as I'd spent around black people running Motown all those years, I couldn't follow it. It just got going quick. Every once in a while, he'd go blah-blah-blah and there would be this huge burst of laughter. It was a real joy to see him get in touch with the real people.

"The next time I saw him after the end of *Bingo* was when I cast him in *The Wiz*. He was just getting married again – one of those marriages – and that presented a problem. Because there was no commercial flight that left Vegas, or wherever he was getting married, I rented a Lear jet and flew him to New York and we put him up at one of the hotels, the Plaza, I think. I called before I went to pick him up to take him to the rehearsal and there was no answer. My heart stopped. So I hurried over and went up to the room and pounded on the door. Still no answer. After the longest time he finally came to the door – we were already late for the rehearsal – and it was clear that he was in a very, very bad mood. He had just come off that NBC television series, an unhappy experience for him, and he was very upset. They had promised him freedom and then censored everything he did. They had three censors sitting there in front of him all the time. Driving downtown to the St. George Hotel, where the re-

124

hearsal was, we were talking about that. And I could see he was brooding. I said, 'Well, you know Richard, here on *The Wiz* it's going to be a very different experience. We're going to do some very exciting things, and everybody's really looking forward to you coming in and working with us.' I could tell he didn't believe me. How to handle it? I figured if I turned him over to Sidney Lumet [the director] first, it might not be so good. Then I had an idea. We had our huge dance rehearsal with four hundred black dancers going on. I said, 'Come on, before we go to the studio, let's take a look at the dancers.' So Richard, wearing a baseball cap and T-shirt, just followed me along very docilely. We walked into the ballroom; they were right in the middle of rehearsing the Emerald City sequence. And they were going full tilt. All of a sudden, some of the dancers in the front row saw me and who was next to me, and they stopped dancing. And it spread. Another five would stop, then twenty, then fifty. Then the whole place stopped. They were just staring at him. Then they broke into spontaneous applause. And he stood up and did a monologue – started doing his black preacher – like, 'We are gathered here today. . . .' They fell down on the floor, they were laughing so hard. And he just suddenly perked right up.

"I've now done two films with him. He was a dream in both. I never had a moment's problem with him. And I've never failed to be amazed by the rapid intelligence that he has. Let me give you one example. After we had finished *Bingo Long,* Richard was staying at the Beverly Hills Hotel, and I went over to talk to him about doing some radio commercials for the movie, which he did. That was in 1976, the year of the Bicentennial, you remember. We were sitting around this bungalow, talking, and I said, 'You know, it's really very disgusting. The Bicentennial has become just another overcommercialized hype. Jesus, the only product that hasn't jumped on the Bicentennial bandwagon is Tampax." Richard immediately picked that up. He jumped up, assumed the voice of your typical unctuous, white-bread announcer, and said, 'Hi there, girls, have you tried Bicentennial Tampax? It's already white and blue, and you can make it red!" And I thought to myself, Christ, in less than a second, he hooked up the Bicentennial, the red, white and blue of the flag, the fact that Tampax wrappings are white and blue, with blue lettering, and that the menstrual flow is red. Red, white and blue. He just tied the whole thing up instantly. In my opinion now, Richard Pryor is training an entire generation of kids that's seeing him in films like *Stir Crazy* and *Silver Streak,* training them from age ten up. They will grow up thinking he's the greatest comedian, the way our generation grew up with Woody Allen. Kids in their teen years now are growing up with Richard Pryor and, as they move through the media generations, they will love him and be loyal to him and applaud this versatility that knows no bounds. He can do anything – films, albums, concerts, and Broadway too. Anything short of opera Richard Pryor can do."

GEORGE CARLIN
(Comedy star)

"One thing I would say about Richard and his impact: I sure would hate to be a young black comic in this country today. Richard established the beachhead and then went inland. What's left to be done in terms of the anger and the perception, and the ability to relate those perceptions verbally in the right language? How can they top him? It's my hunch that a black comic who comes along now will have to be just sheer better by comedy standards, or sheer better by black standards. That's going to be tough. A guy who is only so good, average good, and is black, is going to lose a couple of points just because of Richard. Too bad I'm great at the same time."

JOEL OLIANSKY
(Scriptwriter–Director of the projected
Charlie Parker Story)

"The secret of Richard Pryor's vast appeal? My theory would be that he's very vulnerable, that he looks vulnerable – the big staring eyes and that face that reflects fear, vulnerability. Not weakness, but tenderness. There's an obvious sensitivity there. So, instead of galvanizing an audience away from him, he draws them toward him. You like him. That's the secret. I understand that, when you work with him, he can be suspicious and very on guard. Well, in a way I don't blame him. But that's an occupational hazard when you deal with a star. I've worked with stars before, and to some degree, they're all like that. I talked to one guy who directed Pryor in a film and he gave me this advice: 'Don't ever deal with Richard in a way that somebody has told you to do it. You've got to make up your own number with him. You've got to be yourself, that's all. If somebody has said they did this and that, and it was terrific and worked, don't go and do that. Because he's too fucking smart. He'll realize that they obviously told you how to deal with him.'

"Some people have asked: Does he resent being black? I don't see how any black person would not resent being black in this world, on occasion. Especially in this white-oriented industry. I think every black star who really is a star – from Belafonte and Poitier down to where we are now – has had to face that problem. Then they've had to ask: 'Am I going to take out my resentment for the rest of my life against these motherfuckers because I now have them by the short hairs and they've got to pay me all this money? Or am I going to try to deal with them as equals?' I mean, there's ambivalence in everything. I can't believe they're so well-balanced, any black star, that they don't feel weird and almost schizophrenic in this area. It's impossible to live a rich man's life and not know a lot of white people, because, unfortunately, we've got most of the money. And part of the problem has always been that segregation has been economic as well as racial, and most black people live in neighborhoods that, when you've got Richard's money, you don't live in. Most black people don't live in Hawaii, except those who are native to Hawaii. So, whether he will 'grow away' from his culture I don't know. I think, though, that he must feel certain resentments. I don't see how you can be black and not feel it.

"Of course, Richard's black experience has been different from that of anyone else. Like, say, Redd Foxx. Redd Foxx was not vulnerable in a time when the blacks were just emerging, really. He had emerged long since. He could stand up there and tell you to go fuck yourself and there was something funny and wonderful about Redd Foxx. But he was never going to be lovable as a comedian. He stood out there and told the truth. It was like a glass of ice water after a banquet. It was refreshing and cleared up your head. I think Pryor took a lot of that accuracy and truth, and the language and everything. But with his way of knowing, there was a difference – that vulnerability and that frenzy, unlike Foxx, who was calm as a lake. The perfect difference is when Richard does that whole routine about his monkey dying, and gets teary-eyed about it. Whereas Redd Foxx did one about people swerving their car to avoid hitting an animal. And he said, 'I don't see myself fucking up my thirty thousand dollar Cadillac for no twenty-nine cent cat.' That's the difference between them. Pryor uses the sentiment in a different way. Redd comes on like sentiment is reserved for human beings – you get killed if you're too sentimental, you've got to protect yourself. The mother wit is the guy. He's Harlem. And he's right. Richard Pryor is not Harlem. He's Peoria, Illinois. The difference is that those kids in Peoria hung out on the corner and sang and talked tough. Sure, they knew everything. But, in fact, they were kids who were more romantic. Whatever happened with his parents, Richard didn't have Redd Foxx's childhood. And he made it in show business much earlier than Foxx. Richard was gainfully employed as a comedian when he was barely in his thirties. And that does make a helluva difference. There are also great differences between Richard and Charlie 'Bird' Parker, and that's one reason he's attracted to this role. Because it would stretch him in a different way than he's been stretched. Charlie Parker was a man who was a victim of the American Dream. He lived the life of a bohemian because of the economic condition, but really, at heart, he wished to live like the bourgeoisie. He sought respectability, wished to live a certain kind of life. A good life. Here's a guy, the artistic equal of any musical genius, like Arthur Rubinstein or Andre Watts, who has to scuffle forever. You ask, why didn't he go to Europe and stay there, where they appreciated him? The answer has to be, he wanted to make it in the country where he was born, the country he loved as much as he hated, like any black in America I think, loves this country and hates it in equal measure. He wanted to make it here because here is where, in the American sense, you do make it. You get the money, you get the house. But except as an artist, Bird couldn't make it, couldn't overcome the system; he was too sensitive. It seems to me that Bird almost made a Faustian pact with the Devil, that he knew he was going to die young. And he said, 'Okay, I'll buy that if I can be the greatest musician who ever lived.' And that deal with the Devil was something he was always trying to get out of at the end, but it was too late. The big difference between Charlie Parker and Richard Pryor is that we didn't know how to take care of our geniuses – our black geniuses – in 1955. Maybe we have learned. Because the one thing Richard Pryor won't have to worry about is where his next meal is coming from. That did not happen with Charlie Parker. And it's a great step forward. Richard has made it in American terms – a lot of bread, all the cars you want. All the superficial, surface things that the American Dream promises, Richard achieved. Interior peace can only come from within yourself. But he has been rewarded for his genius in a way that Charlie Parker wasn't. Now the question is whether he can cope with it, enjoy the fruits of all this. But, as I guess Richard would be the first to say, 'There's twenty-two million niggers out there who would love to have the chance to try!' "

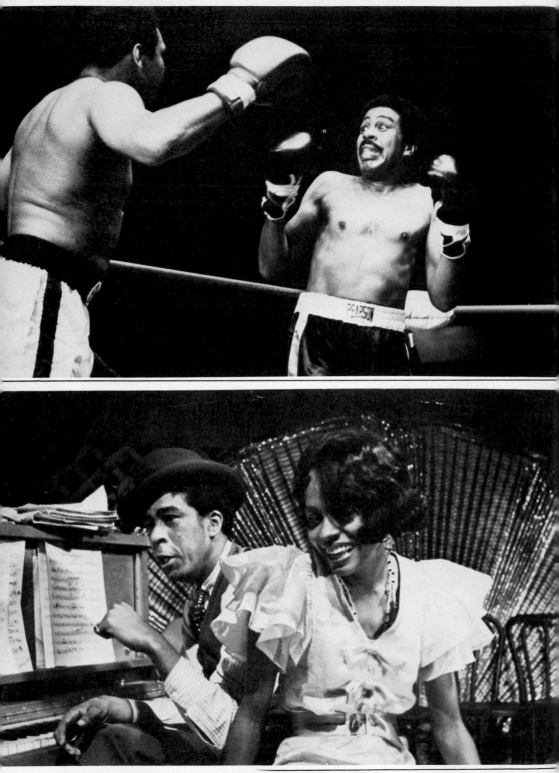

Pryor vs. Ali, in a 1978 Los Angeles fundraiser.

Co-starring with Diana Ross in *Lady Sings the Blues*, 1972.

A skit on NBC with John Belushi.

Flip Wilson, Ruth Buzzi, Pryor, and Buddy Hackett on Flip's TV show in 1973.

On the set of *Stir Crazy* with Gene Wilder.

With Burt Reynolds, as they watch the Leonard-Hearns fight, Las Vegas, September 1981.

In the yard of his home at Sherman Oaks, California, with Barbara Walters six weeks after his accident. July 25, 1980.

With wife Jennifer Lee.

With actress Pam Grier at the 1977 Grammy Awards.

David Bowie and Pryor backstage at *The Johnny Carson Show,* September 5, 1980.

1981.

JOAN RIVERS
(Comedy star)

"*Life* magazine, years ago, was doing an article on me as a comer of the Seventies, you know? Big article. Richard Meryman, who was at that time entertainment director of *Life* and Tommy Thompson, one of his top feature writers, asked, 'What is comedy today?' And we [Rivers and her husband-manager, Edgar Rosenberg] said, 'There is only one man, one person, that you should listen to to describe today's comedy, and that's Richard Pryor.' We took them down to some awful place in the Village where you walked down two steps, I said—both physically and socially—when you walked into that club. He was there—with an audience of five people—and Dick and Tommy were astounded by him, amazed. He would do great improvisational flights of fancy. Just incredible. Funny, funny, funny. And sad. It was acting, it was comedy, it was social comment, it was everything. In the years since, Richard has set such a standard that people now ask where young black comedians can go after Richard Pryor. But it's the same for all comedians. Where does the white comedian go after Lenny Bruce? You just become a comedian. And that's what he has done. I don't think of Richard as a black comic. I think, black, yellow, white or pink, he's the most brillant of our generation. He was the first to say 'nigger,' I'm sure you know that, on the [Johnny] Carson show that time. Which in those days. . . . And he has used all the scatological words that were terribly taboo. I think in the beginning he used them for shock value. And then he woke the audience up and hit them. Now they're going to have to invent some new words.

"Richard is the most brilliant comedy mind working today. What I love about him is that he takes events, things that have happened to people and are so terrible, so horrible, and he makes them funny. And, by making them something to laugh at, he makes you aware of them. Like this whole thing of the boy in the whorehouse – you know what I'm saying? And the guy waiting in the doctor's office, and the penicillin injection, and the pimp on the street. They're brilliant and they're ugly, but he makes them funny, and by the humor he takes you through the ugliness and into the humor and makes you aware of everything. Nobody can touch him today. In my own way, I may do some comparable things, but on a much more shallow scale. I do what's painful for the middle-class woman. That's a whole different thing. He does what's painful for somebody who has really lived through pain. And that's a tremendous accomplishment.

"Richard and I started together in the Village. And at that time I thought he was the only one who touched anything that Lenny Bruce had ever done – that the mind worked like Lenny Bruce's. He took subjects, like Lenny took, that were absolutely *verboten* up to then. Terribly taboo. And he presented them to an audience and made the audience laugh – and think – the way Lenny Bruce did. Lenny broke the door open that we have all walked through, including Richard Pryor. Lenny Bruce was the first one to say all these things, and he suffered for it. Now everybody is into the scatalogical thing. So it does not shock anymore. Everybody's gone one step beyond Bruce now. I wonder where Lenny Bruce would be today? What would Lenny Bruce be talking about today? The times are totally different now. You've got to remember you're dealing with the Flower Children of the Sixties, who were very open and free, and they're now into the Eighties, and they're the ones that love Richard Pryor. That's why I think it's much easier, what he's done. He hasn't had to break through the way Lenny Bruce broke through.

"Also, I think Richard Pryor's being black helped tremendously. Because he was black, I believe, people forgave him a lot more. I think if that had been a white comic [hospitalized after the burning], Teddy Kennedy would not have sent a telegram wishing him well. Being black has allowed Richard Pryor to do what he's doing in comedy. Because of his particular background, growing up in the whorehouse, I think he has deeper sensibilities than any normal, average black child living in the ghetto. His hurts and his scars go deeper than most black ghetto children's do. So he has had more to draw on, more anger – if that's the word – to rise to the surface, to poke fun at. But, as I've always said, 'Show me a comedian with a happy childhood and I'll show you a bad comedian.' Thank God all of us went through horrendous childhoods in one way or another, or we wouldn't be here. In my case, I was very fat, not the most attractive kid. And I came from a family where, if my father made fifty thousand a year, my mother spent seventy thousand. So we were poor. You know what I'm saying? We had bill collectors at a high level. So it was kiting checks, that kind of horror. It made a tremendous scar on a child to have to go to a headmaster's office and say, 'Hold the check.' You don't forget that. You just survive by humor, thank God. You cannot learn to be funny, it has to be there to start with, it had to come out naturally. But when you find that kids think you're funny, you work on it more. You know where my humor comes from? Jews being tortured in the Inquisition! I always feel I could have joked my way out of a concentration camp. And I'm not making a joke when I say that. I would have been the one who survived. I would have been doing the juggling with the Germans. You know what I'm saying? It's a great way to survive. In public, it's too soon to joke about the Holocaust. But I make jokes about the Holocaust, in private. I don't think the Holocaust should be forgotten. And if that makes people remember it, so much the better. Humor is catharsis. It is for me. It is for Richard Pryor. It's saying, 'Look how ugly, look how horrible, look how terrible, look how funny it is.' And while you're laughing you're sympathizing, and, in his case, the sympathy extends, I think, to the next time you look at a poor black child. I think it's wonderful that the whites love him and the blacks love him. But he'll never become a white person's comedian. And I hope he never enjoys the mass appeal of certain comedians. That would take the sting and the excitement and the adventure out of his comedy. Let me tell you, any comedian who pleases everybody is not a good comedian. The minute everybody finds you acceptable, you've passed your prime. When you become a grand old person of comedy – I won't go into names – then it's over for you. You're mush, you're pap, you're not making a point, you're boring. And it's finished.

"I hope Richard Pryor's future includes more and more movies, better movies. So far he hasn't broken any new ground in films the way he broke ground in the spoken comedy. I hope he strives a little higher. Lenny Bruce opened the doors, in spoken comedy, for other comedians, and Richard continues. Now we're all going further. Of course I have my own problems as a woman. For a woman comedian, there's a whole other sensibility there with an audience. If I said 'fuck,' four people would drop dead. I have, every now and again, and they did. And what would happen if I said 'motherfucker'? I think eight would drop dead."

SIDNEY LUMET
(Director of The Wiz)

"I don't agree with those who compare Richard to Lenny Bruce. To me, always – and I saw him a lot – Lenny was basically a fascist. The thinking was fascist. There was an assault on you. It was: 'Up against the wall, motherfucker. Spread your legs. I'm going to beat the shit out of you.' Richard never has that. Richard has such gentleness, basically. He's so questioning. Richard never *tells* you anything. He is funniest when he asks, and he's always asking. His whole character, his whole persona – when he's doing nightclub work, when he's appearing before an audience – is kind of a bemused, befuddled, rather confused guy. He's the one who's always being surprised. In that sense, it's like Chaplin. Things were always happening to Chaplin; things are always happening to Richard. Lenny used to cause things to happen. Lenny was the motor, and Richard is the reactor, to other forces. There's a tremendous difference in their talents, despite the fact that both had enormous shock value. Lenny had shock value because he was *trying* to shock you. Richard has shock value because *he's* shocked. Basically, with Richard, you're seeing the complete man up there. You're not seeing anybody pretending. Now for all I know, and I never knew Lenny Bruce, maybe that was the truth of the man. But I suspect not. I suspect that I was watching an act. With Richard, I'm never aware of watching an act. I think I'm seeing the real person. And if I had to describe him to someone who's never seen him, I don't think I could even begin. How do you describe an original? He's a total original, and the only way to experience it is to see him. The word 'genius' gets kicked around an awful lot, but Richard really is a genius, I think. He's dramatically an extraordinary actor. It's all there. His instinct is so pure. I don't know what kind of training he's had. I would doubt he's ever had any, but it doesn't matter. He can create it on the spur of the moment. And he can keep it. He's totally disciplined. He works within the text when he has to. I don't know where you begin with him, because as far as I'm concerned, there's nothing he cannot do. Before he was cast in *The Wiz* I'd seen him a lot; I'm one of the reasons he's such a box-office hit, because I see everything he does – it's an absolutely unique talent there. The rumored 'unpredictability' didn't happen at all when we worked on *The Wiz*. He worked on a part, like any other actor. He was at work on the character, and the character was alive and clear, and we'd discuss it. I didn't treat it like 'Oh, we're dealing with an inexperienced person here; we've come from a different world, and I better teach him to act.' I absolutely assumed that he was totally trained. There's no way I would ever have been condescending enough to treat him differently than I would another actor. And it turned out to be the exact right thing to do because he was totally at home in acting. He meets that basic artistic requisite of everything, which is 'Use yourself.' And God knows he does.

"When we were doing *The Wiz*, his network television show came out. And he was just totally deballed. He was so tight and tense; and tension is the first thing that kills comedy anyway.

Perhaps he did not realize that commercial TV is not the medium in which he could be relaxed. He's such an optimist. I remember sitting with him and watching one of the shows, maybe the second one. And he kept saying, 'That's funny, that's going to work; that's funny.' And it was quite clear that it wasn't funny. The audience wasn't really laughing. But I don't know that he realized it until it was over. In his own element, of course, he is absolutely unique. Some have talked about the 'outrageousness of his comedy approach.' Well, the most outrageous thing is the fact that it's true, that he doesn't invent anything, that it's full of invention, but completely based on the truth. The use of himself, the use of his own life, is extraordinary. The extreme limit to which he goes not only doesn't shock me, it's part of his brilliance. That's always going to exist. He's always going to be able to break molds, because what comes out of him is not only the truth of his experience, but – and this is why the word 'genius' starts coming into it – what he sees in his experience, as singular as it is, the more specific it gets, the more meaning it has for all of us. The kind of human truth that he hits, in the examination of his own experience, is something that touches every one of us. And it doesn't matter how outrageous that experience is, or how far away the experience is from our own reality, he nevertheless gets a human meaning out of it that affects every single person – and in a time when, really, black entertainers have collapsed, because of the political situation in this country and a million other factors. It's *that*, I think, that keeps Richard up there as a big box-office star, as the force that he is. Because what goes on with him is just so undeniable, and not even the most racist person in the world can deny his impact. He reaches everybody. I don't see his traumatic experience [the fire] as any problem as it affects his comedy. Not at all. He's obviously always been a very self-destructive man. He clearly had better do something about it or he's just not going to live. And, from everything I hear, he's done something about it. I understand he's totally clean now, and straight. And God bless him. His future as an actor is anything he wants. It's all there. And what's interesting is that the more the success comes, he doesn't seem to lose track of what he's out to do. He seems to be holding to it quite clearly. What kind of role would I cast Richard in again? I would cast him in anything from – oh God, you name it – anything from Malcolm X to the Flier in *The Little Prince*. His range is incredible. From an acting point of view, Richard's still untouched."

BRUCE JAY FRIEDMAN
(Novelist; scriptwriter of Stir Crazy*)*

"First, a confession. Filming *Stir Crazy*, Richard was very scrupulous about saying the dialogue as it was written throughout. But that line that everyone quotes, 'Thass right, thass right, we bad' – Richard improvised that himself. That was his. How could I not like it? I loved it. He can improvise anything he wants. That was all Richard, and it was delicious. One hundred percent credit to Richard. I just went along for the ride.

[At one point, during or after *Stir Crazy*, a personality conflict developed between Friedman and Pryor, about which neither cares to elaborate. They resolved their differences later when, after the fire, Pryor tried out new material for his concert film at the Comedy Store in Hollywood and Friedman went to see him there.] We had kind of a personal reunion, a wonderful reunion, backstage. It was very warm – big hugs and kisses – and one of the nicest things that ever happened to me in my life. I couldn't have felt better about the whole thing. We understand each other. The feeling between us is one hundred percent. Any of those negative feelings I might have had are forgotten. It wasn't a scheduled appearance, and I went there two nights before I got to see him. I sat through sixteen lousy comedians on a Friday night, and no Pryor. It took a lot to get me back. But a fellow I was working with on a new picture, Michael Pressman, had just directed Richard in *Some Kind of Hero*, and he promised me Richard would be there. So I went back a second time, despite the memory of those sixteen lousy comedians. You know, whenever you have someone who is a breakthrough comedian, or a breakthrough writer, like Hemingway or whoever, one of the unfortunate aspects of it is that it spawns a whole group of people who take on the outward characteristics but without the essential wit accompanying it – the Hemingway imitators. The Comedy Store was my first exposure to all the new comics. And their comedy is very heavily ethnic, until it finally gets down to a guy who comes out there and starts pissing on Mexicans. In other words, his agent says, 'Well, just piss on a few Mexicans, tell the Jews to fuck off, tell a couple of Polish jokes, and I'll get you on Johnny Carson.' If this was in response to Pryor's stuff, what they failed to take into account is that Richard is probably the most brilliant living social satirist. And his gifts of observation are more acute and precise than those of anybody I know, either as a comic or a writer. So they come out and think all you have to do is piss on the Mexicans and you're funny. The last comic I saw, that's all he did. 'What are you, a Jewish guy? Well, fuck off. Any Mexicans here? Well, up your ass. Take a taco and. . . .' Bullshit. Comics like this guy forget that this has to be accompanied by charm and wit and actual observation. Otherwise it's just name-calling. So it was a fascinating couple of nights I had in that place. Then Richard came out. I've never seen such love communicated to a performer before in my life. Absolutely incredible. Just the announcement that he was there – people were just out of their minds. It wasn't a real big audience, since it wasn't a scheduled performance. But what a reception! Richard was a little bit low-energy, and he was obviously developing some stuff for his concert, but he was pretty wonderful. When he was funny he was awful funny. But there's a kind of a loving, gentle thing that's come over him. And it's both better and worse for the comedy, you know? He was still pretty outrageous when he was outrageous. But there was also a little section there where you could see a kind of generosity or sweetness that hadn't really been present before. It worked. It didn't spoil anything. He explained why he was never going to say 'nigger' again in his act. He said he'd been to Africa, and he sort of had different feelings; he wasn't going to say 'honky,' he wasn't going to say 'nigger.' (He sure as hell still says 'motherfucker'; that didn't change.) He explained his change of attitude; he just took a little time out to talk about his feelings in that department. He said he didn't like that word 'nigger' any more, doesn't want to say it any more. Well, it's like a Jewish comic who does 'kike' material, and everybody gets a giggle every time he says it, but all of a sudden he realizes, 'What is that?' I would never be presumptuous enough to ask Richard directly why he is not using the term 'nigger' any more. But I would say the reason is having more of a sense of himself as a person. You could say his use of the word 'nigger' was a crutch. You know, instant reaction, instant outrageousness, instant freak people out. But he's so much better than that. Also, when you've had an experience that's as traumatizing as his, you sit back and think and wonder about stuff like that.

"Now that whole thing about him 'losing it' and being more mellow is inaccurate. I would say he's just added another dimension, and is just as witty and brilliant as he's always been. While at work on developing material for his concert he did a little bit of stuff, a little piece of business, on the burning. It's almost obligatory, you know. He has a cigarette and he just leans down to somebody in the audience for a light. He pulls back by a hair and all he says is 'careful' – and the place just exploded. The timing was just exquisite. Richard didn't know I was in the audience. But he mentions *Stir Crazy*, and he gets a big response just from that. Then he does about twenty minutes of prison material, stuff that he ran into while making the picture– like two mass murderers fucking. It's really . . . well, if you want to talk about him getting mellow, just forget about that!

"I always think that guys like Richard were born with the gift of being more ferociously honest than anybody else. They don't say anything other people haven't noticed, but they observe it more acutely. And they express things other people are a little nervous or embarrassed about expressing. The funniest guys, to me, are the most honest guys. And that's what gives you that shiver of recognition and makes you laugh. They're just more honest than anyone else. So television, of course, is not the medium for them. I watched some of Richard's TV stuff and it was like Reggie Jackson having to bat blindfolded, you know? Kind of Mickey Mouse. You could see the impulse, but it was always blunted, for obvious reasons. I think he's at his best –thank God I finally got to see him–live. Richard is simply tougher, more incisive, stronger, more lethal than anyone around. He says the unsayable, and that in itself is not automatically an achievement, but he says it with real wit. In his act at the Comedy Store, he, personally, may have been just a little bit softer than before, but not his material. He thanked the people in the audience for all their love and support. Then he said, 'But, then, there were some of you, which I heard about. . . .' And then he lit a match and wiggled it in the air, and he said, 'This is Richard Pryor after his explosion,' or something like that. As he did that little piece of business with the match, he said, 'I heard about some of that shit too.' There's a tiny bit of what I would call reflection in his performance and style now. But I don't know if there's been a great change in him. I have to be straight business about this; I don't really know the man that well, I don't spend much time with him. I just love him. On *Stir Crazy*, I just paid one visit to the set, and spent a little time with Richard, and that was my whole participation in the shooting of the film. When I met him he said, 'They've been telling me you wrote this for me. Is that true or not?' Well, I'm not a fashioner, I've never written anything for anybody; it doesn't work well for me to do that. So I said, 'No, I didn't, but of course I was thrilled when I heard you wanted to play the part.' And he said, 'Well, it's much better that way.'

"Richard is a real major movie star, and, as fine as he was in *Stir Crazy*, *Some Kind of Hero* is the best he's ever been on screen. It's powerful. People come to see Richard so he can make them laugh, which he does a little bit in this, but it's very, very moving and wonderful. Seeing him in this performance, it's as if I'd never seen him before. He's really as close to Chaplin as anybody I've ever seen. This is the first time he's ever gotten a full shot. And, to use a word directors use, his choices in emotional scenes are so incredibly out of sync and yet so wonderful, it's quite amazing. I'm really crazy about him and wish him the best. I'll be watching him; I'm interested in everything he has to say. Richard Pryor's a very special man. I hope we stay friends."

ROBERT KLEIN
(Comedy star)

"There's a parallel between Richard Pryor and myself which he first pointed out many years ago when we became friends at The Improvisation. He observed that we get our impulses similarly; like jazz musicians we think of things on the floor—and then they become material. The fact that we came from opposite ends of the universe is almost irrelevant to that point. In the Improv days, Richard was more advanced than I, a bit older and had been in show business a little longer. He was already doing *The Merv Griffin Show,* which I wanted to do. He was adorable on that show, a delight. He had an unsophisticated political sense, but he knew that he was a black man and he didn't want to Uncle Tom it. So on the show, he stopped being cute and became totally irreverent and unpredictable and militant. And that is not entirely good, but it was entirely natural. He sort of swung all the way the other way. As for his later overuse of scatalogical language, I just think that profanity wears thin sometimes. I wish that some other words could be picked and poked. This is, in a sense, nitpicking, because you're dealing with a brilliant performer, because great comedy can also be un-nerving. I can think of no other person who is as good. His virtuosity is unquestioned. He's so gifted. One of the secrets to his great talent is his ability as an actor. He's first-rate at pretending he's anybody in any given situation. It may very well be that his terrifying accident—while it's unfortunate that it happened—will prove a positive turning point in his life. I want to see more joy in him. The guy is capable of joy. His performances are joyous, perhaps, for the audience. But I'm an optimist and I would like to see, in the middle of all this terror, some more of that.

"Some people may compare him to Lenny Bruce. But they are quite different. The difference is that Lenny Bruce opened up to issues outside himself. His Governor Faubus bit in 1958 or '59, which was so ahead of its time, is one example. Richard does not comment on issues of larger breadth. He goes from the inside out. And the inside is so real and revealing – admitting personal shortcomings, putting your dirty laundry out, and making people laugh at it. But Richard doesn't come in on a world view so much – on segregation, on political issues. And in that sense I think he's not a black Lenny Bruce.

"Certainly Richard is explosive and totally unpredictable; he has shown certain violent tendencies in his life. I personally was never afraid of him, I had no reason to be. He was a sweet guy to me when I knew him. And yet I remember an incident in front of The Improv, where he slapped some girl – girlfriend or something. He didn't hurt the person but it was not a pretty incident. It was one of several incidents. I can remember saying, half-jokingly, 'You're just too dangerous. I'm a middle-class jerk. You make me nervous.' It was my way of scolding him for that slapping incident. But I believe he has this explosiveness, and I think that the comedy has been a very safe outlet for him. He's the kind of guy – you have to think – this guy is not going to die a natural death. On the other hand, there's a beautiful side to him. When I got married nine years ago we flew out to Los Angeles. Our honeymoon was to be a drive up the Coast to San Francisco, along the scenic route on Highway 1 they use for television commercials. As we were driving out Sunset Boulevard toward the ocean, this Porsche comes up alongside and passes us, with Richard sitting shotgun and some grayhaired guy driving. I go, honk, honk, honk, and Richard turns around and sees me and he goes – makes this funny face of his. And he pulls me over and says, 'Hey, you just got married! Come to my house!' And my wife goes, 'Uh-oh, the honeymoon is going to be delayed here.' So we went to his house – on the ocean – for an afternoon snack, which involved brandy and other things. And it was a delightful way to start a honeymoon. I mean, he is like that.

"As I say, I personally never experienced his rougher side. But I think, yes, he has this explosion of unpredictability in him, and probably the comedy is such an outlet that it prevented him from being a much more violent person. And his comedy is changing. He no longer needs to reaffirm his blackness. At the start, not being sophisticated and just working off his emotions and great talent, it was just kind of a roughshod: 'Hey, I'm black' and so forth. I don't think he feels he has to do that any more. Confidence has brought a certain amount of change. He's so in demand and has had to depend on working with so many white people – many of whom he's had to and does trust – so I think his attitude is tempered. I think the issue with respect to him *personally* is really finished. It is not finished with respect to the world at large. Of course, I think he doesn't forget who he is, and won't let anyone else forget it either. And he *does* love to shock. It's kind of getting in your two cents there, and twisting it a little. It's not altogether virtuous. He surely isn't perfect. And if I could mold him, take his great talent and make him the way I want him, it would be a little different than the way it is.

"The fact that Richard is able to express himself so freely now makes him a symbol for free thought and free expression in this country. He certainly has not been co-opted. He never played along unnecessarily. I can't say he struck a perfect balance but now his talent has been realized by everyone. He's accepted on rather universal terms. There's no question that if all this were put back thirty-five years he would have been doing three to five, you know? I don't think the comedy is a product of the time but I believe that the ability to promulgate it to the public at large is definitely a product of the time, a very thankful product of the time, and something Americans should be quite proud of. We should be extolling – investigating rather – our virtues. And this is one of them: to allow someone to get out there and express himself because he makes everyone laugh, no matter what color they are. Now Richard's totally accepted. A performer could not ask for more. It's come to fruition. The man, among the most talented ever, is finally, totally accepted. He can do what he wants, and this, of course, is a great burden on him. What does he do with this mandate? That's very important. And I think that the possibilities are unlimited. With his talent, he could go on forever. It's a cliché, but the only major obstacle to Richard is Richard himself."

LET RICHARD PRYOR HAVE THE LAST word: "I say, 'Allow me to grow.' Nobody can stay the same unless he's Plastic Man. Just watch and see where my growth takes me. Maybe some day folks will say, 'Look at the mother-fucker! He don't say all that shit he used to say, yet he's still saying some funny shit.' That'll be my growth."

Discography

CRAPS
(Feb. 1971)
Laff #A146

PRYOR GOES FOXX HUNTING
(June 1973)
Laff #A170

THAT NIGGER'S CRAZY
(1974)
Reprise REP2287

DOWN–N–DIRTY
(June 1975)
Laff #A184

IS IT SOMETHING I SAID?
(1975)
Reprise REP2285

RICHARD PRYOR MEETS RICHARD & WILLIE & THE S.L.A.
(Jan. 1976)
Laff #A188

BICENTENNIAL NIGGER
(1976)
Reprise WB3114

L.A. JAIL
(1976)
Tiger Lily

"ARE YOU SERIOUS???"
(June 1977)
Laff #A196

RICHARD PRYOR'S GREATEST HITS
(1977)
Warner Bros. WB3057

RICHARD PRYOR LIVE
(1977)
World Sound

WHO ME? I'M NOT HIM
(Nov. 1977)
Laff #A198

BLACK BEN THE BLACK SMITH
(March 1978)
Laff #A200

THE WIZARD OF COMEDY
(Sept. 1978)
Laff #A202

OUTRAGEOUS
(July 1979)
Laff #A206

WANTED: LIVE IN CONCERT
(1979)
Reprise WB3364

INSANE
(Feb. 1980)
Laff #A209

HOLY SMOKE
(Aug. 1980)
Laff #A212

RICHARD PRYOR'S GREATEST HITS
(1980)
Reprise REP6325

REV. DU-RITE
(May 1981)
Laff #A216

Filmography

Compiled by David Ragan

THE BUSY BODY
(1967; Paramount)
Cast: Sid Caesar, Robert Ryan, Anne Baxter, Kay Medford, Godfrey Cambridge, Bill Dana, Ben Blue, Dom DeLuise, George Jessel, Jan Murray, Richard Pryor, Arlene Golonka.
Credits: Producer–Director: William Castle; Screenplay: Ben Starr; Based on a novel by Donald F. Westlake.
101 Minutes.

WILD IN THE STREETS
(1968; American International)
Cast: Shelley Winters, Christopher Jones, Diane Varsi, Ed Begley, Hal Holbrook, Richard Pryor.
Credits: Producer: Samuel Z. Arkoff; Director: Barry Shear; Screenplay and story: Robert Thorn.
96 Minutes.

THE GREEN BERETS
(1968; Warner Bros.–7 Arts)
Cast: John Wayne, David Janssen, Jim Hutton, Aldo Ray, Raymond St. Jacques, Bruce Cabot, Jack Soo, George Takei, Edward Faulkner, Jason Evers, Mike Henry, Craig Jue, Chuck Robertson, Eddy Donno, Rudy Robins, Richard "Cactus" Pryor.
Credits: Producer: Michael Wayne; Directors: John Wayne and Ray Kellogg; Screenplay: James Lee Barrett; Story: Robin Moore; Score: Miklos Rozsa; Song "The Ballad of the Green Berets": Barry Sadler.
141 Minutes.

THE PHYNX

(1970; Warner Bros.)

Cast (listed alphabetically): Patti Andrews, Edgar Bergen, Dick Clark, Xavier Cugat, Cass Daley, Andy Devine, etc., Richard Pryor.

Credits: Producer: Bob Booker; Director: Lee H. Katzin; Screenplay: Stan Cornyn.

91 Minutes.

YOU'VE GOT TO WALK IT LIKE YOU TALK IT OR YOU'LL LOSE THAT BEAT

(1971; JER)

Cast: Zalman King, Allen Garfield, Suzette Green, Richard Pryor.

Credits: Director: Peter Locke.

85 Minutes.

LADY SINGS THE BLUES

(1972; Paramount)

Cast: Diana Ross, Billy Dee Williams, Richard Pryor, Virginia Capers, Scatman Crothers.

Credits: A Motown-Weston-Furie Production; Executive Producer: Berry Gordy; Producers: Jay Weston and James S. White; Director: Sidney J. Furie; Screenplay: Terence McCloy, Chris Clark and Suzanne dePasse; Based on the Billie Holliday autobiography by William Dufty; Music score: Michel Legrand.

144 Minutes.

DYNAMITE CHICKEN

(1972; EYR)

Cast (listed alphabetically): The Ace Trucking Company, Joan Baez, Jim Buckley, Al Capp, Ron Carey, Leonard Cohen, Richard Pryor.

WATTSTAX
(1973; Columbia)

Cast: Isaac Hayes, Staple Singers, Jimmy Jones, Little Milton, Richard Pryor, The Emotions, Albert King, Luther Ingram, Johnnie Taylor, The Dramatics, Kim Weston, Rufus Thomas, Carla Thomas.

Credits: Producers: Larry Shaw and Mel Stuart; Director: Mel Stuart.

100 Minutes.

THE MACK
(1973; Cinerama)

Cast: Max Julien, Don Gordon, Richard Pryor, Juanita Moore.

Credits: Producer: Harvey Bernard; Director: Michael Campus; Screenplay: Robert J. Poole.

110 Minutes.

HIT!
(1973; Paramount)

Cast: Billy Dee Williams, Richard Pryor, Paul Hampton, Gwen Welles.

Credits: Producer: Harry Korshak; Director: Sidney J. Furie; Screenplay: Alan R. Trustman and David S. Wolf.

134 Minutes.

SOME CALL IT LOVING
(1973; CineGlobe)

Cast: Zalman King, Carol White, Tisa Farrow, Richard Pryor.

UPTOWN SATURDAY NIGHT
(1974; Warner Bros.)
Cast: Harry Belafonte, Sidney Poitier, Bill Cosby, Lincoln Kirkpatrick, Roscoe Lee Browne, John Sekka, Ketty Lester, Rosalind Cash, Lee Chamberlin, Richard Pryor, Flip Wilson, Calvin Lockhart, Paula Kelly.
Credits: Producer: Melville Tucker; Director: Sidney Poitier; Screenplay: Richard Wesley.
104 Minutes.

ADIOS AMIGO
(1976; Atlas Films)
Cast: Fred Williamson, Richard Pryor, James Brown, Robert Phillips, Mike Henry, Suhalia Farhat.
Credits: A Po' Boy Production; Writer–Producer–Director: Fred Williamson; Executive Producer: Lee W. Winkler; Music composer–conductor: Luici de Jesus; Performed by: The Blue Infernal Machine.
87 Minutes.

CAR WASH
(1976; Universal)
Cast (listed alphabetically)**:** Franklin Ajaye, Sully Boyar, Richard Brestoff, Carmine Caridi, George Carlin, Prof. Irwin Corey, Ivan Dixon, Bill Duke, Antonio Fargas, Michael Bennell, Arthur French, Lorraine Gary, Darrow Igus, Leonard Jackson, DeWayne Jessie, Lauren Jones, Jack Kehoe, Henry Kingi, Melanie Mayron, Garrett Morris, Clarence Muse, Leon Pinkney, The Pointer Sisters, Richard Pryor, etc.
Credits: Producers: Art Linson and Gary Stromberg; Director: Michael Schultz; Screenplay: Joe Schumacher; Music: Norman Whitfield.
97 Minutes.

THE BINGO LONG TRAVELING ALL-STARS AND MOTOR KINGS
(1976; Universal)

Cast: Billy Dee Williams, James Earl Jones, Richard Pryor, Rico Dawson, Sam (Birmingham) Brison.

Credits: Producer: Rob Cohen; Executive Producer: Berry Gordy; Director: John Badham; Screenplay: Hal Barwood and Matthew Robbins; Based on the novel by William Brashler; Music: William Goldstein; Songs: Ron Miller, William Goldstein, Berry Gordy.

110 Minutes.

SILVER STREAK
(1976; 20th Century-Fox)

Cast: Gene Wilder, Jill Clayburgh, Richard Pryor, Patrick McGoohan, Ned Beatty, Clifton James, Ray Walston, Stefan Gierasch.

Credits: A Miller—Milkis—Colin Higgins Production; Executive Producers: Martin Ransohoff and Frank Yablans; Producers: Thomas L. Miller and Edward K. Milkis; Director: Arthur Hiller; Screenplay: Colin Higgins; Music composer—conductor: Henry Mancini.

113 Minutes.

WHICH WAY IS UP?
(1977; Universal)

Cast: Richard Pryor, Lonette McKee, Margaret Avery, Morgan Woodward, Marilyn Coleman.

Credits: Producer: Steve Krantz; Director: Michael Schultz; Screenplay: Carl Gottlieb and Cecil Brown; Based on the film script of *The Seduction of Mimi* by Lina Wertmuller; Music: Paul Riser and Mark Davis.

94 Minutes.

GREASED LIGHTNING
(1977; Warner Bros.)

Cast: Richard Pryor, Beau Bridges, Pam Grier, Cleavon Little, Vincent Gardenia, Richie Havens, Julian Bond, Earl Hindman, Minnie Gentry, Lucy Saroyan.

Credits: A Third World Cinema Production; Producer: Hannah Weinstein; Executive Producers: Richard Bell and J. Lloyd Grant; Director: Michael Schultz; Screenplay: Kenneth Vose, Lawrence DuKore, Melvin Van Peebles, Leon Capetanos; Music: Fred Karlin.

96 Minutes.

BLUE COLLAR
(1978; Universal)

Cast: Richard Pryor, Harvey Keitel, Yaphet Kotto, Ed Begley Jr., Harry Bellaver, George Memmoli, Lucy Saroyan.

Credits: A TAT Communications Company Production; Executive Producer: Robin French; Producer: Don Guest; Director: Paul Schrader; Screenplay: Paul Schrader and Leonard Schrader; Based on source material by Sydney A. Glass; Music: Jack Nitzsche; Special music arrangements: Ry Cooder.

110 Minutes.

THE WIZ
(1978; Universal)

Cast: Diana Ross, Michael Jackson, Nipsey Russell, Lena Horne, Richard Pryor, Ted Ross, Mabel King.

Credits: A Motown Production; Executive Producer: Ken Harper; Producer: Rob Cohen; Director: Sidney Lumet; Screenplay: Joel Schumacher; Based on the play *The Wiz,* book by William F. Brown, and the book *The Wonderful Wizard of Oz* by Frank L. Baum; Songs: Charlie Smalls; Music adapter—supervisor: Quincy Jones.

133 Minutes.

CALIFORNIA SUITE
(1978; Columbia)
Cast: (four playlets) Jane Fonda and Alan Alda; Maggie Smith and Michael Caine; Walter Matthau, Elaine May and Herbert Edelman; Richard Pryor, Bill Cosby, Gloria Gifford and Sheila Frazier.
Credits: A Ray Stark Production; Producer: Ray Stark; Director: Herbert Ross; Screenplay: Neil Simon (based on his play); Music: Claude Bolling.
103 Minutes.

RICHARD PRYOR IN CONCERT
(1979; Special Event Entertainment)
Cast: Richard Pryor.

THE MUPPET MOVIE
(1979; Archway Film Distributors)
Cast: Jim Henson, Frank Oz, Jerry Nelson, Richard Hunt, Dave Goetz and guest stars Charles Durning, Austin Pendleton, Scott Walker, Edgar Bergen, Milton Berle, Mel Brooks, James Coburn, Dom DeLuise, Elliott Gould, Bob Hope, Madeline Kahn, Carol Kane, Cloris Leachman, Steve Martin, Richard Pryor, Telly Savalas, Orson Welles, Paul Williams.
Credits: An ITC Entertainment Film; A Jim Henson Production; Executive Producer: Martin Starger; Producer: Jim Henson; Co-producer: David Lazer; Director: James Frawley; Screenplay: Jerry Juhl and Jack Burns; Music: Paul Williams.
98 Minutes.

IN GOD WE TRUST

(1980; Universal)

Cast: Marty Feldman, Peter Boyle, Louise Lasser, Richard Pryor, Andy Kaufman, Wilfred Hyde-White, Severn Darden.

Credits: A Howard West/George Shapiro Production; Producers: Howard West and George Shapiro; Executive Producer: Norman T. Herman; Director: Marty Feldman; Screenplay: Marty Feldman and Chris Allen; Associate Producer: Lauretta Feldman; Music: John Morris; Song "Good For God": Harry Nilsson.

97 Minutes.

WHOLLY MOSES!

(1980; Columbia)

Cast: Dudley Moore, Laraine Newman, James Coco, Paul Sand, Jack Gilford, Dom DeLuise, John Houseman, Madeline Kahn, David L. Lander, Richard Pryor.

Credits: Producer: Freddie Fields; Executive Producer: David Begelman; Director: Gary Weis; Screenplay: Guy Thomas; Music: Patrick Williams.

109 Minutes.

STIR CRAZY

(1980; Columbia)

Cast: Gene Wilder, Richard Pryor, George Sanford Brown, Jobeth Williams.

Credits: A Hannah Weinstein Production; Producer: Hannah Weinstein; Director: Sidney Poitier; Executive Producer: Melville Tucker; Screenplay: Bruce Jay Friedman; Music: Tom Scott.

111 Minutes.

BUSTIN' LOOSE

(1981; Universal)

Cast: Richard Pryor, Cicely Tyson.

Credits: Producers: Richard Pryor and Michael S. Glick; Executive Producer: William Greaves; Director: Oz Scott; Screenplay: Roger L. Simon; Based on an idea by Richard Pryor; Music: Mark Davis; Songs (composed and sung by): Roberta Flack.

94 Minutes.

SOME KIND OF HERO

(1982; Paramount)

Cast: Richard Pryor, Margot Kidder, Ray Sharkey, Ronny Cox, Lynne Moody, Olivia Cole, Matt Clark, Tony Ponzini.

Credits: Producer: Howard W. Koch; Director: Michael Pressman; Screenplay: Robert Boris and James Kirkwood; Based on a novel by James Kirkwood.